Living Liturgy™

for Extraordinary Ministers
of Holy Communion

for Extraordinary Ministers of Holy Communion

Year C • 2010

Joyce Ann Zimmerman, CPPS
Kathleen Harmon, SNDdeN
Christopher W. Conlon, SM

LITURGICAL PRESS
Collegeville, Minnesota

www.litpress.org

Design by Ann Blattner. Art by Annika Nelson.

ISSN 1933-3129

ISBN 13: 978-0-8146-3005-1

Presented to

_____

in grateful appreciation
for ministering as an
Extraordinary Minister
of
Holy Communion

_____

_____

(date)

USING THIS RESOURCE

By baptism we are all made members of the Body of Christ. Extraordinary ministers of Holy Communion are called to serve the Christian community by ministering the Body and Blood of Christ to the Body of Christ. Rather than a "status symbol" in the liturgical community, these ministers are servants of the servants, as Jesus himself showed us at the Last Supper. They are called "extraordinary" not because of any personal worthiness or honor but because the "ordinary" ministers of Holy Communion are bishops, priests, deacons, or instituted acolytes. In the typical parish situation, however, large numbers of the faithful come forward for Communion, and so in most cases lay members of the parish are designated as "extraordinary" ministers so that this part of the Mass does not become disproportionately long.

Preparing for this ministry

As with all ministry, extraordinary ministers of Holy Communion must prepare themselves for their ministry. This book is intended to be a guide and resource for that preparation. Each Sunday and some key feast days are laid out with the gospel text (or a shortened version of it), prayer, and reflections to help the Communion minister prepare each week, even when he or she is not scheduled for ministry. Some of the language of the text implies a group is present for the preparation; these texts are conveniently worded for when two or more extraordinary ministers gather for preparation, or for when these texts are shared in the context of the rite of Holy Communion with the homebound and sick.

Holy Communion for the homebound and sick

Jesus' preaching of the Good News in the gospel is made visible by his many and varied good works on behalf of others. Perhaps more than any other group, Jesus reaches out with his healing touch to those who are sick, and this compassionate ministry continues today in the life of the church. One of the many blessings of parishes that have extraordinary ministers of Holy Communion is that parishioners who are sick or homebound or those in hospitals and other care centers can share in the liturgical life of parishes more frequently. These ministers are reminded that the sick and suffering share in a special way in Jesus' passion. The ministers can bring hope and consolation and the strength of the Bread of Life to those who seem cut off from active participation in parish life.

Adapting this resource for Holy Communion for the homebound and sick
It is presumed that each Communion minister is familiar with the rites for Communion with the sick. There is a brief rite for those in hospitals or other care centers; this shorter rite is used when the circumstances would not permit the longer rite. The longer rite is used in ordinary circumstances and includes a Liturgy of the Word preceding the Communion rite. When using the longer rite, the opening and closing prayer of this book would nicely round out the beginning and end of the service; the gospel is conveniently included to proclaim the Word, and a reflection (also included in this book) may be shared.

Privilege and dignity
It is indeed a unique blessing to serve members of the parish as extraordinary ministers of Holy Communion, both at the parish Mass and by bringing Communion to the sick and homebound. The parish's presence through ministry to the sick and homebound is a particular sign of their dignity as members of the Body of Christ. The Communion minister is in a unique position to bring hope and comfort to those who may find little in life to comfort them. May this ministry always be a sign of Jesus' great love and compassion for all his Father's beloved children!

Our God is coming, not just in our anticipation of Christmas as we begin Advent, but at the end of time when Christ will come in great power to save us. We pause a few moments during our busy lives to open our hearts to the signs of Christ's coming among us . . .

Prayer

God of wonder and might, you have redeemed us by the saving mystery of your divine Son. Help us to be vigilant for his many comings and to welcome him with eagerness to serve him more faithfully. We ask this through Christ our Lord. **Amen**.

Gospel (Luke 21:25-28, 34-36)

Jesus said to his disciples: "There will be signs in the sun, the moon, and the stars, and on earth nations will be in dismay, perplexed by the roaring of the sea and the waves. People will die of fright in anticipation of what is coming upon the world, for the powers of the heavens will be shaken. And then they will see the Son of Man coming in a cloud with power and great glory. But when these signs begin to happen, stand erect and raise your heads because your redemption is at hand.

"Beware that your hearts do not become drowsy from carousing and drunkenness and the anxieties of daily life, and that day catch you by surprise like a trap. For that day will assault everyone who lives on the face of the earth. Be vigilant at all times and pray that you have the strength to escape the tribulations that are imminent and to stand before the Son of Man."

Brief Silence

For Reflection

The source of the vigilance the gospel admonishes is found in these two actions: God's call and our response. The redemption at hand promised in the gospel is God's work, but it also calls for a response from us—we must do our part by growing in love, living in ways pleasing to God, and being faithful to the teachings of Christ. Moreover, the very discernment of signs of the Lord's presence is already a response, already a factor in the end-time judgment. We have nothing to fear when we live as if the end time were now, as if Christ is present in all his glory now.

One sign of the Son of Man's presence is that we are growing in love. Despite appearances to the contrary (disaster and destruction generated both by natural forces and human choices), God's plan and purpose are directed toward redemption and life. We need to read the right signs—new life in the midst of seeming destruction, the glory of the Son of Man coming into the darkness, the love of Christ growing in our hearts.

✦ My life—as Christ's Eucharist for others—reveals Christ's coming when I . . . I nourish and strengthen others until Christ comes in glory whenever I . . .

Brief Silence

Prayer

Gracious God, from the very beginning of creation you desired life in abundance for us humans made in your divine image. Be with us as we begin Advent, help love to grow in our hearts, and remove any obstacles from us that may keep us from growing in our love for you. We ask this through Christ our Lord. **Amen**.

Our lives are constantly filled with the ups and downs, the mountains and valleys, of everyday living that challenge us to keep focused on the God who comes to save us. We pause now to recognize God's presence . . .

Prayer

God of history, your word brings truth and life. Strengthen us so that our voices may cry out a message of salvation, hope, and peace to all the ends of the earth. We ask this through Christ our Lord. **Amen**.

Gospel (Luke 3:1-6)

In the fifteenth year of the reign of Tiberius Caesar, when Pontius Pilate was governor of Judea, and Herod was tetrarch of Galilee, and his brother Philip tetrarch of the region of Ituraea and Trachonitis, and Lysanias was tetrarch of Abilene, during the high priesthood of Annas and Caiaphas, the word of God came to John the son of Zechariah in the desert. John went throughout the whole region of the Jordan, proclaiming a baptism of repentance for the forgiveness of sins, as it is written in the book of the words of the prophet Isaiah: / *A voice of one crying out in the desert: / "Prepare the way of the Lord, / make straight his paths. / Every valley shall be filled / and every mountain and hill shall be made low. / The winding roads shall be made straight, / and the rough ways made smooth, / and all flesh shall see the salvation of God."*

Brief Silence

For Reflection

How often do we humans move in very circuitous ways? If we want to drive to the top of a steep mountain, going straight up usually doesn't get us there—we use switchbacks so the grade isn't so steep. Sometimes we go out of our way to avoid other people, especially when there is ill will between them and us. The gospel for this Sunday, contrary to our sometimes roundabout ways, gives us clear instructions: make straight our path to the Lord. The gospel also makes clear the means to make that path straight: repentance and forgiveness.

God's salvation is revealed in repentance (our work) and forgiveness (God's work). The meandering paths and winding roads of our lives are straightened and the valleys filled and mountains brought low when our lives are characterized by attitudes of repentance. To repent means to change one's mind, one's life; this is how we reach the fullness that is promised and our true home: by increasing our love for one another. Our work of repentance is a matter of turning ourselves toward the God who embraces us in mercy and forgiveness and welcomes us home.

✦ A way that the Eucharist reveals the "salvation of God" for me is . . .

Brief Silence

Prayer

Loving God, you call us into your presence. Help us to make our winding roads straight, leading us into your loving embrace and everlasting life. We ask this through Christ our Lord. **Amen**.

Mary, conceived without sin, faithfully said yes to God. We pause to examine our own faithfulness in saying yes to God as well as marvel at Mary's faithfulness . . .

Prayer

God of salvation, you prepared Mary from the very beginning of her life as a fitting and pure vessel to receive the life of your divine Son. May we also be fitting vessels to receive your divine indwelling and be ever faithful in bringing your presence to all those we meet. We ask this through Christ our Lord. **Amen**.

Gospel (Luke 1:26-38)

The angel Gabriel was sent from God to a town of Galilee called Nazareth, to a virgin betrothed to a man named Joseph, of the house of David, and the virgin's name was Mary. And coming to her, he said, "Hail, full of grace! The Lord is with you." But she was greatly troubled at what was said and pondered what sort of greeting this might be. Then the angel said to her, "Do not be afraid, Mary, for you have found favor with God. Behold, you will conceive in your womb and bear a son, and you shall name him Jesus. He will be great and will be called Son of the Most High, and the Lord God will give him the throne of David his father, and he will rule over the house of Jacob forever, and of his Kingdom there will be no end." But Mary said to the angel, "How can this be, since I have no relations with a man?" And the angel said to her in reply, "The Holy Spirit will come upon you, and the power of the Most High will overshadow you. Therefore the child to be born will be called holy, the Son of God. And behold, Elizabeth, your relative, has also conceived a son in her old age, and this is the sixth month for her who was called barren; for nothing will be impossible for God." Mary said, "Behold, I am the handmaid of the Lord. May it be done to me according to your word." Then the angel departed from her.

Brief Silence

For Reflection

Mary participated in God's work of salvation in these ways: she was overshadowed by the Holy Spirit, the child born to her is the Son of God, and she said yes to God. We, too, each have our "annunciation" by which the Spirit dwells within us, we bear Christ in the world today, and we are called to speak an ongoing yes to God. In these ways we, like Mary, participate in God's work of salvation. Our "annunciations" are in the ordinary, everyday circumstances that present us with the choice to say yes to God.

God's announcement of a divine word to us probably won't come in such an extraordinary way as an angel appearing to us. God's word does come to us through the ordinary people and circumstances of our everyday lives. It comes to us at liturgy and when we take personal time to pray. It comes to us at times of repentance and forgiveness. The challenge is to recognize God's word and respond with a faithful yes, as Mary responded to God and lived her whole life in cooperation with the divine plan of salvation. As Mary bore the Son of God, we are also to bear Christ within us—by our faithfully saying yes to God.

✦ Like Mary, I have been invited through my eucharistic ministry to participate in God's work of salvation for others when . . .

Brief Silence

Prayer

God of promises, you are faithful in offering divine life to those who say yes to your holy will. Help us to say yes to you with eager hearts, ready to serve you in one another. We ask this through Christ our Lord. **Amen.**

The gospel for this Sunday asks three times: "What should we do?" We pause to ask the same question of ourselves: in this busy time before Christmas, what is the Lord asking of us? . . .

Prayer

God of Good News, you fill us with expectation as we anticipate celebrating the birth of your Son. Help us to slow down our racing lives and ponder what it is you ask of us. We ask this through Christ our Lord. **Amen**.

Gospel **(Luke 3:10-18)**

The crowds asked John the Baptist, "What should we do?" He said to them in reply, "Whoever has two cloaks should share with the person who has none. And whoever has food should do likewise." Even tax collectors came to be baptized and they said to him, "Teacher, what should we do?" He answered them, "Stop collecting more than what is prescribed." Soldiers also asked him, "And what is it that we should do?" He told them, "Do not practice extortion, do not falsely accuse anyone, and be satisfied with your wages."

Now the people were filled with expectation, and all were asking in their hearts whether John might be the Christ. John answered them all, saying, "I am baptizing you with water, but one mightier than I is coming. I am not worthy to loosen the thongs of his sandals. He will baptize you with the Holy Spirit and fire. His winnowing fan is in his hand to clear his threshing floor and to gather the wheat into his barn, but the chaff he will burn with unquenchable fire." Exhorting them in many other ways, he preached good news to the people.

Brief Silence

For Reflection

In the gospel three groups of people ask the same question: "What should we do?" John exhorts them to define their obligations in right relation to others, just as John himself defines his role in relation to Jesus. The gospel, further, pivots on the people's "expectation." To whom were their expectations led? The Christ (the Messiah), yes, but also to another "who"—our neighbor. The "good news" is that our relationships with others make visible our relation to Jesus. "What should we do?"

John answers them by using himself as the model for the ultimate answer to the question, "What should we do?" John denies being "the Christ" himself and announces that "one mightier than I is coming." Just like John, our lives are about others. And by being about others, we actually exceed ourselves and point people to the presence of Christ. Thus, the explicit question about what we are to do points to our natural desire for finding the ultimate One. We define ourselves not in terms of what we do but who we are in relation to Other and others. The *relationship* to others is the key, not what we or they do.

✦ If I could ask John the Baptist, what should I do? he would say to me . . .

Brief Silence

Prayer

Loving God, you sent your Spirit to baptize us with fire. Fill us with expectation and help us to be eager to discover the many ways Christ comes to us. We ask this through Christ our Lord. **Amen**.

Believing the angel Gabriel, Mary set out to visit her cousin Elizabeth who, "filled with the Holy Spirit," announced that her Lord is present. To prepare for our celebration of the Savior's coming, let us welcome God's presence now . . .

Prayer

O God, you filled the holy women Mary and Elizabeth with the Holy Spirit. Help us to appreciate with grateful hearts that the same Spirit is present within each of us, filling us with wonder and joy. We ask this through Christ our Lord. **Amen**.

Gospel (Luke 1:39-45)

Mary set out and traveled to the hill country in haste to a town of Judah, where she entered the house of Zechariah and greeted Elizabeth. When Elizabeth heard Mary's greeting, the infant leaped in her womb, and Elizabeth, filled with the Holy Spirit, cried out in a loud voice and said, *"Blessed are you among women, and blessed is the fruit of your womb.* And how does this happen to me, that the mother of my Lord should come to me? For at the moment the sound of your greeting reached my ears, the infant in my womb leaped for joy. Blessed are you who believed that what was spoken to you by the Lord would be fulfilled."

Brief Silence

For Reflection

The gospel, in fact, announces two "incarnations": Jesus in the womb of Mary, and the Holy Spirit who filled Elizabeth. Although Elizabeth extols Mary for her belief in what would happen to her, it was also Elizabeth's belief that enabled her to conceive John as well as recognize the presence of the Savior in her midst through Mary. Our own belief enables the "incarnation" within us of both the presence of the risen Christ and the Holy Spirit. Blessed are they, and blessed are we to whom God comes and within whom God dwells.

On this last Sunday before Christmas we are gently led into the depths of the Christmas mystery. Already on this Sunday we are reminded that his life was one of obedience to his Father, which meant offering his body for our salvation. Mary and Elizabeth show us the way to *our* being overshadowed by the Spirit by their offering of their own bodies in cooperating with God's plan of salvation. Always our encounters with God lead to an annunciation of God's presence, an incarnation of that presence within each of us, and an unprecedented blessedness as we share in the very life of God.

✦ I recognize Christ and the Holy Spirit "incarnated" in others when . . . and in myself when . . .

Brief Silence

Prayer

Gracious God, you nourish us with faith and joy. Open our hearts to the mystery of the incarnation, that we may bring Jesus' presence to all those we meet. We ask this through Christ our Lord. **Amen**.

We celebrate once again the birth of the incarnate Son of God, Jesus our Savior. As our waiting has come to an end, may we open our hearts to God's loving presence to us as beloved sons and daughters . . .

Prayer

God of light and majesty, from the beginning your Word was life and joy. As we celebrate the birth of this Word made flesh, open our hearts to the fullness of grace you offer us. We ask this through Christ our Lord. **Amen.**

Gospel (John 1:1-5, 9-14; from the Mass During the Day)

In the beginning was the Word, / and the Word was with God, / and the Word was God. / He was in the beginning with God. / All things came to be through him, / and without him nothing came to be. / What came to be through him was life, / and this life was the light of the human race; / the light shines in the darkness, / and the darkness has not overcome it.

The true light, which enlightens everyone, was coming into the world.

He was in the world, / and the world came to be through him, / but the world did not know him. / He came to what was his own, / but his own people did not accept him.

But to those who did accept him he gave power to become children of God, to those who believe in his name, who were born not by natural generation nor by human choice nor by a man's decision but of God.

And the Word became flesh / and made his dwelling among us, / and we saw his glory, / the glory as of the Father's only Son, / full of grace and truth.

Brief Silence

For Reflection

How lofty a meditation this gospel offers us on this Christmas Day when we celebrate the birth of Jesus! From the very beginning this new Life we celebrate was God, was the source of created life, was the light that dispelled the darkness of nothingness. But John doesn't stay with these lofty thoughts. He also affirms that "the Word became flesh and made his dwelling among us." This divine One came to dwell among us not as a deity but as one who gave himself in suffering and death for our salvation.

But the act of self-giving of this divine One comes full circle, for from "his fullness we have all received." Indeed, through him we "become children of God." The One who took on our human flesh and dwelled among us is the "Father's only Son," he who chooses to be present to us in such an intimate way that we ourselves are made more perfectly into his image and likeness through the "grace and truth" he brings. The glad tidings this birth brings is the Good News of salvation, the Good News that God dwells among us and is present to us in a whole new way.

✦ God's self-gift to us is the divine Son. My own self-gift to others is . . .

Brief Silence

Prayer

God of creation, your Son dwells among us and gives us life and peace. Be with us as we strive to dispel the darkness around us and bring the light of Christ to all we meet. We ask this through Christ our Lord. **Amen**.

The church, God's holy family, is called to model her values and behaviors on those of Jesus, Mary, and Joseph. Let us open ourselves to this great mystery and resolve to grow in the holiness to which we have been called . . .

Prayer

All holy God, your divine Son Jesus sought to be in your holy temple. Help us always to seek you in wisdom and knowledge, in prayer and presence, in truth and life. We ask this through Christ our Lord. **Amen**.

Gospel (Luke 2:41-52)

Each year Jesus' parents went to Jerusalem for the feast of Passover, and when he was twelve years old, they went up according to festival custom. After they had completed its days, as they were returning, the boy Jesus remained behind in Jerusalem, but his parents did not know it. Thinking that he was in the caravan, they journeyed for a day and looked for him among their relatives and acquaintances, but not finding him, they returned to Jerusalem to look for him. After three days they found him in the temple, sitting in the midst of the teachers, listening to them and asking them questions, and all who heard him were astounded at his understanding and his answers. When his parents saw him, they were astonished, and his mother said to him, "Son, why have you done this to us? Your father and I have been looking for you with great anxiety." And he said to them, "Why were you looking for me? Did you not know that I must be in my Father's house?" But they did not understand what he said to them. He went down with them and came to Nazareth, and was obedient to them; and his mother kept all these things in her heart. And Jesus advanced in wisdom and age and favor before God and man.

Brief Silence

For Reflection

The gospel opens with a telling detail: the Holy Family goes to Jerusalem each year at Passover, the Jewish feast that recalls Israel's identity as the family of God's people. Mary and Joseph consciously formed Jesus in the traditions and memories of the family of Israel. We, too, belong to a larger family, for we are the children of God. This larger family is not something abstract but very concrete: our being members of God's holy family is expressed in our own nuclear families, where we build our identities from the traditions of goodness and values that we pass on from generation to generation.

The model that the Holy Family provides us is one of fidelity to traditions and obedience to who they were. They teach us that holiness means we are "in [our] Father's house," because there we learn our religious traditions and form the memories that make us who we are as members of the larger family of God. They teach us that we really belong to God, and everything about our living must reflect that we are most at home "in [our] Father's house."

✦ I model holiness by the manner in which I distribute Holy Communion by . . .

Brief Silence

Prayer

God our Father, you call us to your presence and shower us with the holiness of your divine life. May our communion with you strengthen us to reach out to others with your presence and love. We ask this through Christ our Lord. **Amen**.

This festival honors Mary, the Mother of God, who bore the divine Son within her womb. The mystery of the incarnation is so great that Mary "kept all these things, reflecting on them in her heart." Let us pause a moment for our own reflection on this great mystery . . .

Prayer

Life-giving God, as Mary gave birth to the divine Son, through him you offer all of us life and grace. Be with us as we follow Jesus and seek to be life-bearers for all those we meet. We ask this through Christ our Lord. **Amen**.

Gospel (Luke 2:16-21)

The shepherds went in haste to Bethlehem and found Mary and Joseph, and the infant lying in the manger. When they saw this, they made known the message that had been told them about this child. All who heard it were amazed by what had been told them by the shepherds. And Mary kept all these things, reflecting on them in her heart. Then the shepherds returned, glorifying and praising God for all they had heard and seen, just as it had been told to them.

When eight days were completed for his circumcision, he was named Jesus, the name given him by the angel before he was conceived in the womb.

Brief Silence

For Reflection

The salvation events that the incarnation unleashed are neither easy to understand nor to embrace. Yet the shepherds did hear the message of the angels and then they made it known. Mary, in turn, heard their Good News, took it into her heart, and reflected on it. Mary shows us the way: we, too, must adopt a contemplative stance before God and the mystery of salvation. Mary's ongoing yes to God wasn't really very easy at all. The only way she continued to be faithful was that she took a contemplative stance: reflecting, pondering, praying.

The mystery of the incarnation that Mary models for us is that God's life dwells within each of us. But in our busy, everyday living we can easily lose sight of that Life within us. We can easily get distracted from a contemplative stance that helps us appreciate God's abiding presence to us. It is only by making conscious effort to ponder, like Mary, the way we live and how God's grace is guiding us that we are able to face the inevitable difficulties of daily living with the sureness of blessing and strength.

✦ If I am to imitate and develop Mary's reflective stance found in the gospel, I must . . .

Brief Silence

Prayer

God of life and salvation, you shower your grace and light upon us. Strengthen us to be faithful to your gracious presence and to make known that presence to others. We ask this through Christ our Lord. **Amen**.

The magi followed the star to the newborn King and offered him homage. Let us prepare ourselves to offer God homage always by examining how well we have followed God's Light in our own lives . . .

Prayer

O God who guides and protects, you manifested the Light of your divine Son to all the nations. Help us to search diligently for Christ's presence among us, and to respond with the gift of our own service. We ask this through Christ our Lord. **Amen**.

Gospel (Matt 2:1-12)

When Jesus was born in Bethlehem of Judea, in the days of King Herod, behold, magi from the east arrived in Jerusalem, saying, "Where is the newborn king of the Jews? We saw his star at its rising and have come to do him homage." When King Herod heard this, he was greatly troubled, and all Jerusalem with him. Assembling all the chief priests and the scribes of the people, he inquired of them where the Christ was to be born. They said to him, "In Bethlehem of Judea, for thus it has been written through the prophet: / *And you, Bethlehem, land of Judah, / are by no means least among the rulers of Judah; / since from you shall come a ruler, / who is to shepherd my people Israel."* / Then Herod called the magi secretly and ascertained from them the time of the star's appearance. He sent them to Bethlehem and said, "Go and search diligently for the child. When you have found him, bring me word, that I too may go and do him homage." After their audience with the king they set out. And behold, the star that they had seen at its rising preceded them, until it came and stopped over the place where the child was. They were overjoyed at seeing the star, and on entering the house they saw the child with Mary his mother. They prostrated themselves and did him homage.

Then they opened their treasures and offered him gifts of gold, frankincense, and myrrh. And having been warned in a dream not to return to Herod, they departed for their country by another way.

Brief Silence

For Reflection

The point of this Epiphany gospel is even more amazing than the imaginative details it includes: God chooses to manifest the mystery of Christ Jesus to all the nations. This, of course, includes each of us today: we are to search for the Christ as well as manifest his presence for others. Note that our task-response is not only to search for the Christ among us but also to manifest that divine presence. In other words, we are to *be* the revelation of his presence. We are to *be* the story of the manifestation of Christ to all the world.

The light of the glory of God's presence is all around us. Unlike the magi, we don't have to undertake an arduous journey. We need only to do two things: be single-minded about seeking God's presence, and arm ourselves with whatever we need to reach our journey's end. The real challenge of the gospel is that we do not seek the light outside of ourselves, but within. We ourselves have become the story; we ourselves are the guiding light; we ourselves manifest divine presence.

✦ I am radiant with the Light who is Christ when I distribute Holy Communion because . . .

Brief Silence

Prayer

O God, you give us the wondrous gift of your divine Son. Help us to give you the gift of faithful hearts, offering homage to you through the good we do. We ask this through Christ our Lord. **Amen**.

Jesus' identity as beloved Son of God was manifested at his baptism. Through our own baptism we share in this divine identity, which is manifested in the good works of our own lives. We ask God to strengthen us to be faithful disciples of Jesus . . .

Prayer

God our Father, your Spirit came upon Jesus at his baptism when you announced that Jesus is your beloved Son. May that same Spirit enlighten us, help us to live faithfully our own baptismal identity as your beloved children, and help us to do good works that are pleasing to you. We ask this through Christ our Lord. **Amen**.

Gospel (Luke 3:15-16, 21-22)

The people were filled with expectation, and all were asking in their hearts whether John might be the Christ. John answered them all, saying, "I am baptizing you with water, but one mightier than I is coming. I am not worthy to loosen the thongs of his sandals. He will baptize you with the Holy Spirit and fire."

After all the people had been baptized and Jesus also had been baptized and was praying, heaven was opened and the Holy Spirit descended upon him in bodily form like a dove. And a voice came from heaven, "You are my beloved Son; with you I am well pleased."

Brief Silence

For Reflection

The gospel speaks of two baptisms. The first is the event this feast celebrates: the baptism Jesus received at the hands of John. The second is the baptism that we receive "with the Holy Spirit and fire." Jesus' baptism revealed him as "beloved Son"; our own baptism reveals us as ones who are saved, renewed, justified, and heirs of eternal life. This feast, then, is an epiphany not only of who Jesus is but also of who we are.

We are baptized with the Spirit, who is the divine presence within us. We are also baptized with fire that burns within us so that we are ignited with ardor, commitment, intensity, energy, drive toward a goal—by the very goodness of our lives, being a faithful divine presence for others. Our baptism, then, is a dynamic and energetic embracing of our own graced identity as God's own beloved children, which is expressed through a gospel way of life. The fire with which we are baptized surely must make us eager to do what is good.

✦ Jesus heard who he was ("beloved Son") when he prayed; I realize and remember who I am in faith when I . . .

Brief Silence

Prayer

Lord God, you send the fire of the Holy Spirit to strengthen us. Help us to live our identity as your beloved children, bringing joy and peace to all those we meet. We ask this through Christ our Lord. **Amen**.

Jesus performed his first public sign at the wedding feast at Cana. We pause to reflect on the signs of Jesus' glory in our own lives and to ask God during our prayer to increase our belief . . .

Prayer

Caring God, your Son Jesus was obedient to his mother Mary's wishes and saved the wedding couple from embarrassment. Help us to always be obedient to your holy will and to be gracious to all those we meet. We ask this through Christ our Lord. **Amen**.

Gospel (John 2:1-11)

There was a wedding at Cana in Galilee, and the mother of Jesus was there. Jesus and his disciples were also invited to the wedding. When the wine ran short, the mother of Jesus said to him, "They have no wine." And Jesus said to her, "Woman, how does your concern affect me? My hour has not yet come." His mother said to the servers, "Do whatever he tells you." Now there were six stone water jars there for Jewish ceremonial washings, each holding twenty to thirty gallons. Jesus told them, "Fill the jars with water." So they filled them to the brim. Then he told them, "Draw some out now and take it to the headwaiter." So they took it. And when the headwaiter tasted the water that had become wine, without knowing where it came from—although the servers who had drawn the water knew—, the headwaiter called the bridegroom and said to him, "Everyone serves good wine first, and then when people have drunk freely, an inferior one; but you have kept the good wine until now." Jesus did this as the beginning of his signs at Cana in Galilee and so revealed his glory, and his disciples began to believe in him.

Brief Silence

For Reflection

Why does John begin with a wedding story? What, really, is the wedding? What, really, is the sign? This first manifestation of why Jesus came among us summarizes his whole saving mission, and so John uses this occasion at the beginning of Jesus' public life to give us an overview of the meaning and purpose of Jesus' whole life. All Jesus' life and actions are directed toward his saving work culminating in his death and resurrection—and our response to this is "to believe in him." Our believing is our own action of entering into Jesus' saving work. The wedding feast was an opportunity for epiphany and belief.

John uses the wedding as a metaphor to manifest to us that there is new wine among us. The readings taken together intimate that the marriage is between heaven and earth, divinity and humanity, God and us. The sign is how obedience leads to glory, dying to rising, believing to abundance. The purpose of using wedding imagery runs deep: the sign "revealed [Jesus'] glory." If water changed to wine can reveal Jesus' glory, how much more can changed hearts reveal it!

✦ Those who have been living signs (Eucharist) of Jesus' glory for me are . . .

Brief Silence

Prayer

God of glory, you reveal yourself to us each time we celebrate Eucharist and receive your Son's Body and Blood. Help us to change our hearts into those more perfectly attuned to you and to be ever willing to reveal your presence to others. We ask this through Christ our Lord. **Amen**.

Jesus announced that the word he read in the synagogue was fulfilled in him. Let us open ourselves to God's word and pray that it will be fulfilled in each of us . . .

Prayer

O God of creating word, Jesus revealed himself as your Word fulfilled in him. Help us to be ever more attentive to your word as proclaimed in Holy Scripture, and may it be fulfilled through our good deeds. We ask this through Christ our Lord. **Amen**.

Gospel (Luke 1:1-4; 4:14-21)

Since many have undertaken to compile a narrative of the events that have been fulfilled among us, just as those who were eyewitnesses from the beginning and ministers of the word have handed them down to us, I too have decided, after investigating everything accurately anew, to write it down in an orderly sequence for you, most excellent Theophilus, so that you may realize the certainty of the teachings you have received.

Jesus returned to Galilee in the power of the Spirit, and news of him spread throughout the whole region. He taught in their synagogues and was praised by all.

He came to Nazareth, where he had grown up, and went according to his custom into the synagogue on the sabbath day. He stood up to read and was handed a scroll of the prophet Isaiah. He unrolled the scroll and found the passage where it was written: / *The Spirit of the Lord is upon me, / because he has anointed me / to bring glad tidings to the poor. / He has sent me to proclaim liberty to captives / and recovery of sight to the blind, / to let the oppressed go free, / and to proclaim a year acceptable to the Lord.* / Rolling up the scroll, he handed it back to the attendant and sat down, and the eyes of all in the synagogue looked intently at him. He said to them, "Today this Scripture passage is fulfilled in your hearing."

Brief Silence

For Reflection

In this Sunday's gospel, Jesus reads out loud to the people in the Nazareth synagogue. The hearers must have *heard*, for after Jesus' proclamation in the synagogue, they "looked intently at him." What were they expecting from Jesus? An explanation of what they had just heard, yes. But Jesus moves his hearers beyond receiving mere explanation of the word to encountering him as the Word made flesh.

The synagogue hearers' expectations were fulfilled in two ways: *hearing* God's word and *encountering* God's word in the very person of Jesus. In the very proclamation Jesus also announces his saving mission: to meet the needs of the poor, the captives, the blind, the oppressed. He identifies himself with the word that makes a difference, changes lives, fulfills expectations. Jesus' word is an active word that brings the "glad tidings" of God's care for us to life. Our own hearing and encountering the Word today invites us to participate in these saving deeds as, through us, the Word continues to be made flesh.

✦ I live with integrity the words I announce to communicants, "Body/Blood of Christ," when . . .

Brief Silence

Prayer

Caring God, you heal those who suffer and free those shackled by human weakness. Help us to enflesh your word in our world today, and through us help others encounter your saving presence. We ask this through Christ our Lord. **Amen**.

Jesus was sent to announce the Good News of salvation to Jews and Gentiles alike. Let us open ourselves to the wideness of God's offer of salvation . . .

Prayer

O God, you sent your Son to fulfill the promise of salvation. Help us to withstand any opposition we might have to announcing and living the Gospel. We ask this through Christ our Lord. **Amen**.

Gospel (Luke 4:21-30)

Jesus began speaking in the synagogue, saying: "Today this Scripture passage is fulfilled in your hearing." And all spoke highly of him and were amazed at the gracious words that came from his mouth. They also asked, "Isn't this the son of Joseph?" He said to them, "Surely you will quote me this proverb, 'Physician, cure yourself,' and say, 'Do here in your native place the things that we heard were done in Capernaum.'" And he said, "Amen, I say to you, no prophet is accepted in his own native place. Indeed, I tell you, there were many widows in Israel in the days of Elijah when the sky was closed for three and a half years and a severe famine spread over the entire land. It was to none of these that Elijah was sent, but only to a widow in Zarephath in the land of Sidon. Again, there were many lepers in Israel during the time of Elisha the prophet; yet not one of them was cleansed, but only Naaman the Syrian." When the people in the synagogue heard this, they were all filled with fury. They rose up, drove him out of the town, and led him to the brow of the hill on which their town had been built, to hurl him down headlong. But Jesus passed through the midst of them and went away.

Brief Silence

For Reflection

This Sunday's gospel continues Jesus' teaching in the synagogue, and he speaks words of truth. The gospel challenges us to stand pat on the truth of God's word, even to stake our lives on it—as Jesus did. God is clear on the divine purpose: salvation for all at all costs, even if this means the life of the divine Son.

As long as Jesus announces glad tidings, the crowd responds positively. But when Jesus challenges their narrowness with the examples of Elijah's and Elisha's outreach to Gentiles (Sidon and Syria), they grow furious. The response of the crowd registers increasing resistance—from amazement (at his "gracious words") to skepticism ("Isn't this the son of Joseph?") to fury (they wanted "to hurl him down headlong" from "the brow of the hill"). Jesus challenged the crowd because the Good News is always broader than selective preferences or limited understanding—yes, salvation would be for Gentiles as well as Jews. While the gospel is always Good News, it is not always comfortable because it ever stretches us beyond where we are now.

✦ My distributing Holy Communion stretches me beyond narrowness to the wide reach of God's saving embrace when . . .

Brief Silence

Prayer

O saving God, you extend to us health and mercy even when we don't ask. Be with us as we strive to be faithful to living the Good News, and bring us to everlasting life. We ask this through Christ our Lord. **Amen**.

**In the gospel Jesus
teaches the crowds and
calls Peter, James, and
John to follow him. Let us
pause to hear what Jesus
teaches us and to follow
him more faithfully . . .**

Prayer

O God, you call followers of Jesus to announce the Good News of
salvation. Help us to hear the demands of that call, to open ourselves to your grace, and to serve faithfully. We ask this through
Christ our Lord. **Amen**.

Gospel (Luke 5:1-11)

While the crowd was pressing in on Jesus and listening to the word of
God, he was standing by the Lake of Gennesaret. He saw two boats
there alongside the lake; the fishermen had disembarked and were
washing their nets. Getting into one of the boats, the one belonging to
Simon, he asked him to put out a short distance from the shore. Then
he sat down and taught the crowds from the boat. After he had finished speaking, he said to Simon, "Put out into deep water and lower
your nets for a catch." Simon said in reply, "Master, we have worked
hard all night and have caught nothing, but at your command I will
lower the nets." When they had done this, they caught a great number
of fish and their nets were tearing. They signaled to their partners in
the other boat to come to help them. They came and filled both boats so
that the boats were in danger of sinking. When Simon Peter saw this,
he fell at the knees of Jesus and said, "Depart from me, Lord, for I am a
sinful man." For astonishment at the catch of fish they had made seized
him and all those with him, and likewise James and John, the sons of
Zebedee, who were partners of Simon. Jesus said to Simon, "Do not be
afraid; from now on you will be catching men." When they brought
their boats to the shore, they left everything and followed him.

Brief Silence

For Reflection

What precipitated the radical response of the first disciples who "left everything and followed" Jesus? Clearly, Jesus' words and actions. To fishermen who had labored fruitlessly all night, Jesus tells them to try again and leads them to a great catch. To a sinful Peter who considers himself unworthy of Jesus' company, Jesus says, "follow me" and transforms his life's purpose. More than one miracle has occurred in this gospel.

Jesus "taught the crowds." The miracle of the great catch makes concrete the Good News of Jesus' teaching: God's intervention overturning the futility of mere human work, the super abundance of God's actions on our behalf, the invitation to follow in Jesus' footsteps. The miracle of the catch is the bridge to the second miracle: hearing the Good News and living it. The miracle enabled the disciples to see more deeply into the truth of Jesus' teaching. It's the power of Jesus' Good News that drew them to follow him. Today we are the miracle that makes the Good News visible when we allow God to work in and through us.

✦ My encounters with Jesus in the Body of Christ have changed me from . . . to . . .

Brief Silence

Prayer

God of miracles and Good News, you lavishly pour upon us your goodness and truth. Help us to make the Good News of salvation visible through the good we do for others. We ask this through Christ our Lord. **Amen**.

In this gospel we hear Luke's version of the Beatitudes. Let us pause during our busy lives to take sufficient time to reflect on how we have lived our blessedness . . .

Prayer

Blessed be God who blesses us with all good things! Help us, O God, to reach out to those who find it difficult to recognize their blessings, and lead them to your compassion and care. We ask this through Christ our Lord. **Amen**.

Gospel (Luke 6:17, 20-26)

Jesus came down with the Twelve and stood on a stretch of level ground with a great crowd of his disciples and a large number of the people from all Judea and Jerusalem and the coastal region of Tyre and Sidon. And raising his eyes toward his disciples he said: / "Blessed are you who are poor, / for the kingdom of God is yours. / Blessed are you who are now hungry, / for you will be satisfied. / Blessed are you who are now weeping, / for you will laugh. / Blessed are you when people hate you, / and when they exclude and insult you, / and denounce your name as evil / on account of the Son of Man. / Rejoice and leap for joy on that day! Behold, your reward will be great in heaven. For their ancestors treated the prophets in the same way. / But woe to you who are rich, / for you have received your consolation. / Woe to you who are filled now, / for you will be hungry. / Woe to you who laugh now, / for you will grieve and weep. / Woe to you when all speak well of you, / for their ancestors treated the false prophets in this way."

Brief Silence

For Reflection

In this gospel Luke seems to be exalting the downtrodden simply because they are downtrodden, and cursing the comfortable simply because they are comfortable. While it is true that God has special care for the poor and downtrodden, it is equally true that having possessions is not in itself cause for condemnation. What really is at the heart of this gospel is the manner of life that makes present the kingdom and assures us that our "reward will be great in heaven." The model of this manner of life and the source of the blessedness it brings is Jesus himself.

All who open themselves to the favor that God grants are blessed. First, then, comes God's grace, favor, graciousness. From this comes a relationship with God and our own acknowledgment that we have been chosen by God, blessed by him. Then comes a manner of living that is consistent with our relationship. The "kingdom of God" is ours when our living is in line with Jesus, when all our actions are "on account of the Son of Man." Our reward, indeed, is great—because it is God who blesses.

✦ By recognizing that each communicant is blessed, I am able to . . .

Brief Silence

Prayer

O good God, you bless us abundantly and keep us in your care. Increase in our hearts our gratitude for the many blessings you have given us, and lead us unfailingly toward eternal life. We ask this through Christ our Lord. **Amen**.

We begin Lent not as somber people, but as sober people seeking to root out all that hinders us from becoming closer to God and each other. We pause to place ourselves in God's compassionate embrace . . .

Prayer

God of mercy and compassion, you call us to repentance and conversion. Be with us on our Lenten journey, that we may be faithful to our penance and turn our lives more perfectly toward you. We ask this through Christ our Lord. **Amen**.

Gospel (Matt 6:1-6, 16-18)

Jesus said to his disciples: "Take care not to perform righteous deeds in order that people may see them; otherwise, you will have no recompense from your heavenly Father. When you give alms, do not blow a trumpet before you, as the hypocrites do in the synagogues and in the streets to win the praise of others. Amen, I say to you, they have received their reward. But when you give alms, do not let your left hand know what your right is doing, so that your almsgiving may be secret. And your Father who sees in secret will repay you.

"When you pray, do not be like the hypocrites, who love to stand and pray in the synagogues and on street corners so that others may see them. Amen, I say to you, they have received their reward. But when you pray, go to your inner room, close the door, and pray to your Father in secret. And your Father who sees in secret will repay you.

"When you fast, do not look gloomy like the hypocrites. They neglect their appearance, so that they may appear to others to be fasting. Amen, I say to you, they have received their reward. But when you fast, anoint your head and wash your face, so that you may not appear to be fasting, except to your Father who is hidden. And your Father who sees what is hidden will repay you."

Brief Silence

For Reflection

Jesus counsels us three times in the gospel to give alms, pray, and fast "in secret" where only God knows what we are doing. "In secret," as used in the gospel, raises a question about the motivation for our acts of Lenten penitence. In the gospel Jesus seems to ask us to undertake penance without any of the usual motivation we like, especially "the praise of others," which is so powerfully moving. Our strongest motivation for undertaking Lenten penance, surely, is the deepening of our relationships. Lent directs us inward to self-transformation, which opens us to new relationships with God and each other. Any transformation presupposes that we set right our relationships. In other words, our Lenten practices include the kind of inward renewal that changes how we relate to God and others. Changed behaviors and doing good for others flow from our changed relationships. We are motivated to undertake Lenten practices because they lead us to transformation. Our conversion is possible because of God's gift of new life, because of the community that sustains us, because we grow in love for God and each other.

✦ During this Lent the relationships I need to change are . . . This will change how I do my ministry in that . . .

Brief Silence

Prayer

Loving God, you call us to conversion of heart so that we may grow in our love for you and each other. Increase in us our resolve to do penance, and help our love to grow so that we may journey faithfully toward eternal life. We ask this through Christ our Lord. **Amen**.

In the gospel the Spirit leads Jesus into the desert to be tempted. We don't need to travel to a physical desert to be tempted—we find our desert in the demands of everyday living. Let us ask God to pardon us for the times we have given in to temptation . . .

Prayer

God of mercy and forgiveness, you give us this time of renewal so that we may see truthfully into our hearts. Strengthen us to overcome the temptations that come our way and to draw closer to you during this Lent. We ask this through Christ our Lord. **Amen**.

Gospel (Luke 4:1-13)

Filled with the Holy Spirit, Jesus returned from the Jordan and was led by the Spirit into the desert for forty days, to be tempted by the devil. He ate nothing during those days, and when they were over he was hungry. The devil said to him, "If you are the Son of God, command this stone to become bread." Jesus answered him, "It is written, *One does not live on bread alone*." Then he took him up and showed him all the kingdoms of the world in a single instant. The devil said to him, "I shall give to you all this power and glory; for it has been handed over to me, and I may give it to whomever I wish. All this will be yours, if you worship me." Jesus said to him in reply, "It is written: / *You shall worship the Lord, your God, / and him alone shall you serve*." Then he led him to Jerusalem, made him stand on the parapet of the temple, and said to him, "If you are the Son of God, throw yourself down from here, for it is written: / *He will command his angels concerning you, to guard you, /* and: / *With their hands they will support you, / lest you dash your foot against a stone.*" / Jesus said to him in reply, "It also says, *You shall not put the Lord, your God, to the test.*" When the devil had finished every temptation, he departed from him for a time.

Brief Silence

For Reflection

Jesus was "led by the Spirit into the desert . . . to be tempted." Each temptation put to him by the devil involved some misguided personal gain: seeking easy solutions to human hungers, pursuing "power and glory," defying death. By resisting these temptations, Jesus shows us that our true gain is not found in satisfying ourselves, but in something better—utter fidelity to God. Temptations always face us with the choice between personal gain and something even better: the goodness and holiness that comes from serving God and doing good for others. This same choice between self-satisfaction and fidelity to God frees us, like Jesus, to be who we are meant to be, persons "led by the Spirit."

Like Jesus, temptations and our very resistance to them strengthens us in our choices for goodness and holiness. In making these choices we are continually choosing who we want to be: those who faithfully serve God by doing good for others. Temptations' lure to self-satisfaction is overcome by an even stronger lure: growth in holiness and transformation into ever more beloved sons and daughters of God.

✦ I am most prone to temptation when . . . I am best able to resist temptation when . . .

Brief Silence

Prayer

Compassionate God, you look beyond our weakness to call us to holiness. Help us to grow in your grace this Lent, that one day we may stand everlastingly before your majesty and holiness. We ask this through Christ our Lord. **Amen**.

In this gospel we witness Jesus transfigured in glory. We pause to reflect on the times when we have closed our eyes to this glory because of sin, and we ask God's pardon and mercy . . .

Prayer

Glorious God, you gave Peter, James, and John a glimpse of the glory that rightfully belongs to your divine Son. Draw us to Jesus' presence so that we may listen to his words of salvation and one day attain a fuller share in his glory. We ask this through Christ our Lord. **Amen**.

Gospel (Luke 9:28b-36)

Jesus took Peter, John, and James and went up the mountain to pray. While he was praying his face changed in appearance and his clothing became dazzling white. And behold, two men were conversing with him, Moses and Elijah, who appeared in glory and spoke of his exodus that he was going to accomplish in Jerusalem. Peter and his companions had been overcome by sleep, but becoming fully awake, they saw his glory and the two men standing with him. As they were about to part from him, Peter said to Jesus, "Master, it is good that we are here; let us make three tents, one for you, one for Moses, and one for Elijah." But he did not know what he was saying. While he was still speaking, a cloud came and cast a shadow over them, and they became frightened when they entered the cloud. Then from the cloud came a voice that said, "This is my chosen Son; listen to him." After the voice had spoken, Jesus was found alone. They fell silent and did not at that time tell anyone what they had seen.

Brief Silence

For Reflection

Luke's account of the transfiguration event is the only one that includes the necessity of the passion on the journey to glory ("his exodus that he was going to accomplish in Jerusalem"). To share in the glory of Jesus, disciples must walk the journey of Jesus: offer their very lives for the sake of others. These three apostles were privileged to awaken from sleep to see Jesus' transfigured glory. But they clearly missed the most important point: this transfigured glory foreshadows his risen glory. Luke's insight is that glory always presupposes embracing passion.

Jesus' transfiguration—in all its glory—cannot erase the stark reality of self-offering. Simply put, glory only comes through embracing the passion. This is the paradox of the paschal mystery: that something as desirable as a share in Jesus' transfigured glory comes only through our embrace of something as demanding as dying to self for the good of others. We have to come down off the mountain and walk our own journey through death to glory.

✦ My manner of distributing Holy Communion helps others experience their share in Jesus' transfigured glory when . . .

Brief Silence

Prayer

God of the resurrection, you clothed your Son in glory as he was praying. Help us to be faithful to prayer, and to one day share in the glory of eternal life. We ask this through Christ our Lord. **Amen**.

In this Sunday's gospel Jesus lays before us the choice to repent or perish. We pause now to acknowledge our lack of repentance and ask God to pardon and heal us . . .

Prayer

Patient God, you call us to repentance and shower upon us your mercy. Grant us strength of choice so that we may repent of all that takes us from you. We ask this through Christ our Lord. **Amen**.

Gospel (Luke 13:1-9)

Some people told Jesus about the Galileans whose blood Pilate had mingled with the blood of their sacrifices. Jesus said to them in reply, "Do you think that because these Galileans suffered in this way they were greater sinners than all other Galileans? By no means! But I tell you, if you do not repent, you will all perish as they did! Or those eighteen people who were killed when the tower at Siloam fell on them—do you think they were more guilty than everyone else who lived in Jerusalem? By no means! But I tell you, if you do not repent, you will all perish as they did!"

And he told them this parable: "There once was a person who had a fig tree planted in his orchard, and when he came in search of fruit on it but found none, he said to the gardener, 'For three years now I have come in search of fruit on this fig tree but have found none. So cut it down. Why should it exhaust the soil?' He said to him in reply, 'Sir, leave it for this year also, and I shall cultivate the ground around it and fertilize it; it may bear fruit in the future. If not you can cut it down.'"

Brief Silence

For Reflection

The first two events reported in the gospel involve tragic death, and Jesus uses these tragedies to make absolute that unless we repent, we, too, will die. Then in the parable of the fig tree, Jesus reveals the patience of God with us, despite our slowness to repent. This is God's work of mercy: to take what is almost dead and coax it to new life. This is our work of repentance: to turn from sinfulness toward God's transforming mercy.

Jesus redirects the people from idle speculation about the meaning of the tragic fate of others to the serious work of their own repentance. Basking in the graciousness of the new life God offers us does not mean that because God gives us everything needed for our journey toward salvation, we ourselves don't need to cooperate with God to "cultivate" and "fertilize" our spiritual lives. We grumble our way through life—we judge others, fail to live up to our baptismal commitments, do not heed all the warnings given us. Jesus is quite clear in his message: "bear fruit" or be "cut . . . down." Repent or perish.

✦ The repentance I need to do in order to make my ministry more faithful is . . .

Brief Silence

Prayer

O God, you are the giver of all good things. Help us to repent, bear fruit, and one day enjoy everlasting life with you. We ask this through Christ our Lord. **Amen**.

In the parable of the prodigal son, we encounter God as the merciful Father who always welcomes back repenting children with forgiveness and feasting. To prepare ourselves to celebrate the eucharistic feast, let us repent of our sinfulness . . .

Prayer

Astonishing God, you surprise us with your great mercy and an invitation to your feast. Help us to live in such a way that we hunger only for you, and quickly return to you when we stray. We ask this through Christ our Lord. **Amen**.

Gospel (Luke 15:1-3, 11-32)

Tax collectors and sinners were all drawing near to listen to Jesus, but the Pharisees and scribes began to complain, saying, "This man welcomes sinners and eats with them." So to them Jesus addressed this parable: "A man had two sons, and the younger son said to his father, 'Father give me the share of your estate that should come to me.' So the father divided the property between them. After a few days, the younger son collected all his belongings and set off to a distant country where he squandered his inheritance on a life of dissipation. When he had freely spent everything, a severe famine struck that country, and he found himself in dire need. So he hired himself out to one of the local citizens who sent him to his farm to tend the swine. And he longed to eat his fill of the pods on which the swine fed, but nobody gave him any. Coming to his senses he thought, 'How many of my father's hired workers have more than enough food to eat, but here am I, dying from hunger. I shall get up and go to my father and I shall say to him, "Father, I have sinned against heaven and against you. I no longer deserve to be called your son; treat me as you would treat one of your hired workers.'" So he got up and went back to his father. While he was still a long way off, his father caught sight of him, and was filled with compassion. He ran to his son, embraced him and kissed him. His son said to him, 'Father, I have sinned against heaven and against you; I no longer deserve to be called your son.' But his father ordered his servants, 'Quickly bring the finest robe and put it on him; put a ring on his finger and sandals on his feet. Take the fattened calf and slaughter it. Then let us celebrate with a feast, because this son of mine was dead, and has come to life again; he was lost, and has been found.' Then the celebration began. Now the older son had been out in the field and, on his way back, as he neared the house, he heard the sound of music and dancing. He called one of the servants and asked what this might mean. The servant said to him, 'Your brother has returned and your father has slaughtered the fattened calf because he has him back safe and sound.' He became angry, and when he refused to enter the house, his father came out and pleaded with him. He said to his father in reply, 'Look, all these years I served you and not once did I disobey your orders; yet you never gave me even a young goat to feast on with my friends. But when your son returns who swallowed up your property with prostitutes, for him you slaughter the fattened calf.' He said to him, 'My son, you are here with me always; everything I have is yours. But now we must celebrate and rejoice, because your brother was dead and has come to life again; he was lost and has been found.'"

Brief Silence

For Reflection

The gospel begins with the Pharisees and scribes complaining
that Jesus welcomes and eats with sinners—how little they understand God! So Jesus tells a parable. When the prodigal son came
"to his senses" and returned home, the most he hoped from his
father was to be given a place as a servant and adequate food to
eat. But the merciful father was prodigious: he embraced him,
clothed him in dignity, and honored him with a feast. Sinners
though we are, our merciful Father still longs to embrace and celebrate with us. We have only to return to him.

Forgiveness brings us to accept others (and ourselves) as weak
human beings who often hurt others and cause them anguish.
We are like the prodigal father when we are compassionate and
forgiving toward those who have harmed us. Then we are like our
merciful God who treats us in just this same way.

✦ The father is the one who goes out to both sons and invites
them to the feast. Imitating this compassionate father, the one I
need to invite back to the feast is . . .

Brief Silence

Prayer

God of joy, you overlook our weakness and invite us to share in
your everlasting feast. May we always turn toward you and be
open to your transforming offer of mercy and forgiveness. We ask
this through Christ our Lord. **Amen**.

Jesus does not condemn the adulterous woman in this gospel but commands her to sin no more. Let us pause to acknowledge our own sinfulness and receive God's mercy . . .

Prayer

God of mercy and forgiveness, you humble us in our sinfulness and exalt us when we repent. Help us to acknowledge truthfully our wrongdoings and resolve to sin no more. We ask this through Christ our Lord. **Amen**.

Gospel (John 8:1-11)

Jesus went to the Mount of Olives. But early in the morning he arrived again in the temple area, and all the people started coming to him, and he sat down and taught them. Then the scribes and the Pharisees brought a woman who had been caught in adultery and made her stand in the middle. They said to him, "Teacher, this woman was caught in the very act of committing adultery. Now in the law, Moses commanded us to stone such women. So what do you say?" They said this to test him, so that they could have some charge to bring against him. Jesus bent down and began to write on the ground with his finger. But when they continued asking him, he straightened up and said to them, "Let the one among you who is without sin be the first to throw a stone at her." Again he bent down and wrote on the ground. And in response, they went away one by one, beginning with the elders. So he was left alone with the woman before him. Then Jesus straightened up and said to her, "Woman, where are they? Has no one condemned you?" She replied, "No one, sir." Then Jesus said, "Neither do I condemn you. Go, and from now on do not sin any more."

Brief Silence

For Reflection

The crowd brings before Jesus a woman caught in adultery, condemns her, and demands her life. Jesus doesn't condemn the woman. He does condemn her act ("do not sin any more"), and then calls her to repent and choose a new way of living. Lent calls us to the same kind of encounter with Jesus so that we face our own sinfulness, hear his invitation to embrace a new way of living, and make the right choice. Central to this gospel is not simply the adulterous woman or even the crowd that came to a realization of their own sinfulness. Taking a central place is an encounter with Jesus, who calls us to repentance and offers us divine mercy. We are quick to condemn each other; Jesus assures us, "Neither do I condemn you." We need only to acknowledge our sinfulness and turn toward God. This is repentance. It rests in divine encounter and results in truth: our sinfulness, God's mercy, the promise of new life.

✦ Looking on the face of communicants draws me to extend greater compassion and mercy toward others by . . .

Brief Silence

Prayer

God of mercy and new life, you judge us with compassion and truth. Help us to repent of our sinfulness, turn from our selfish ways, and come to share in everlasting life with you. We ask this through Christ our Lord. **Amen**.

Let us begin this solemn Holy Week by resolving to enter into the mystery we celebrate with fervor, admit our sinfulness, and ask for God's strength and mercy . . .

Prayer

Holy God, you have been present to us during these Lenten days. As we enter into Holy Week, may we surrender ourselves to the dying and rising mystery of your Son with fervor and whole-hearted resolve. We ask this through Christ our Lord. **Amen**.

Gospel (Luke 23:1-49 [Longer Form: Luke 22:14–23:56])

The elders of the people, chief priests and scribes, arose and brought Jesus before Pilate. They brought charges against him, saying, "We found this man misleading our people; he opposes the payment of taxes to Caesar and maintains that he is the Christ, a king." Pilate asked him, "Are you the king of the Jews?" He said to him in reply, "You say so." Pilate then addressed the chief priests and the crowds, "I find this man not guilty." But they were adamant and said, "He is inciting the people with his teaching throughout all Judea, from Galilee where he began even to here."

On hearing this Pilate asked if the man was a Galilean; and upon learning that he was under Herod's jurisdiction, he sent him to Herod who was in Jerusalem at that time. Herod was very glad to see Jesus; he had been wanting to see him for a long time, for he had heard about him and had been hoping to see him perform some sign. He questioned him at length, but he gave him no answer. The chief priests and scribes, meanwhile, stood by accusing him harshly. Herod and his soldiers treated him contemptuously and mocked him, and after clothing him in resplendent garb, he sent him back to Pilate. Herod and Pilate became friends that very day, even though they had been enemies formerly. Pilate then summoned the chief priests, the rulers, and the people and said to them, "You brought this man to me and accused him of inciting the people to revolt. I have conducted my investigation in your presence and have not found this man guilty of the charges you have brought against him, nor did Herod, for he sent him back to us. So no capital crime has been committed by him. Therefore I shall have him flogged and then release him."

But all together they shouted out, "Away with this man! Release Barabbas to us."—Now Barabbas had been imprisoned for a rebellion that had taken place in the city and for murder.—Again Pilate addressed them, still wishing to release Jesus, but they continued their shouting, "Crucify him! Crucify him!" Pilate addressed them a third time, "What evil has this man done? I found him guilty of no capital crime. Therefore I shall have him flogged and then release him." With loud shouts, however, they persisted in calling for his crucifixion, and their voices prevailed. The verdict of Pilate was that their demand should be granted. So he released the man who had been imprisoned for rebellion and murder, for whom they asked, and he handed Jesus over to them to deal with as they wished.

As they led him away they took hold of a certain Simon, a Cyrenian, who was coming in from the country; and after laying the cross on him, they made him carry it behind Jesus. A large crowd of people followed Jesus, including many women who mourned and lamented him. Jesus turned to them and said, "Daughters of Jerusalem, do not weep for me; weep instead for yourselves and for your children for indeed, the days are coming when people will say, 'Blessed are the barren, the wombs that never bore and the breasts that never nursed.' At that time people will say to the mountains, 'Fall upon us!' and to the hills, 'Cover us!' for if these things are done when the wood is green what will happen when it is dry?" Now two others, both criminals, were led away with him to be executed.

When they came to the place called the Skull, they crucified him and the criminals there, one on his right, the other on his left. Then Jesus said, "Father, forgive them, they know not what they do." They divided his garments by casting lots. The people stood by and watched; the rulers, meanwhile, sneered at him and said, "He saved others, let him save himself if he is the chosen one, the Christ of God." Even the soldiers jeered at him. As they approached to offer him wine they called out, "If you are King of the Jews, save yourself." Above him there was an inscription that read, "This is the King of the Jews."

Now one of the criminals hanging there reviled Jesus, saying, "Are you not the Christ? Save yourself and us." The other, however, rebuking him, said in reply, "Have you no fear of God, for you are subject to the same condemnation? And indeed, we have been condemned justly, for the sentence we received corresponds to our crimes, but this man has done nothing criminal." Then he said, "Jesus, remember me when you come into your kingdom." He replied to him, "Amen, I say to you, today you will be with me in Paradise."

It was now about noon and darkness came over the whole land until three in the afternoon because of an eclipse of the sun. Then the veil of the temple was torn down the middle. Jesus cried out in a loud voice, "Father, into your hands I commend my spirit"; and when he had said this he breathed his last.

Here all kneel and pause for a short time.

The centurion who witnessed what had happened glorified God and said, "This man was innocent beyond doubt." When all the people who had gathered for this spectacle saw what had happened, they returned home beating their breasts; but all his acquaintances stood at a distance, including the women who had followed him from Galilee and saw these events.

Brief Silence

For Reflection

On five occasions in Luke's passion account, Jesus is declared innocent (three times by Pilate, once by the Good Thief, once by the centurion at the foot of the cross). Jesus died, not because of guilt, but because of his infinitely compassionate love for us. Even in the midst of great suffering, he extended his compassion to others (to the servant whose ear was cut off, to the weeping women, to the good thief). His compassion was so total that he willingly emptied himself even to the point of death. We enter into this holiest week of the year, praying that our self-emptying for the good of others could be so total! We pray that our compassion may increase and abound so that we have the same utter confidence in God's presence and care as Jesus.

Jesus' innocence conditions how he approaches others with compassion. His innocence is an invitation and challenge for us to take up our own cross and participate in self-emptying dying—not just during this holiest of weeks, but during every week of our lives.

✦ The manner of my distributing Holy Communion encourages others to greater compassion when . . .

Brief Silence

Prayer

Compassionate God, you invite us to enter into this holiest of weeks with arms extended to receive your presence and saving mercy. Strengthen us to carry our own cross, that one day we may enter into eternal glory. We ask this through Christ our Lord. **Amen**.

Each time that we gather to celebrate Eucharist, we experience Jesus' servant-love for us, ritualized on Holy Thursday in the washing of feet. Let us prepare for the celebration of these three days of the paschal Triduum by opening our hearts to hear God's word and be fed at God's table . . .

Prayer

God of love, your Son left us his very Body and Blood as a memorial of his self-giving sacrifice. Help us to always hunger for the only food that nourishes us to eternal life. We ask this through Christ our Lord. **Amen**.

Gospel (John 13:1-15)

Before the feast of Passover, Jesus knew that his hour had come to pass from this world to the Father. He loved his own in the world and he loved them to the end. The devil had already induced Judas, son of Simon the Iscariot, to hand him over. So, during supper, fully aware that the Father had put everything into his power and that he had come from God and was returning to God, he rose from supper and took off his outer garments. He took a towel and tied it around his waist. Then he poured water into a basin and began to wash the disciples' feet and dry them with the towel around his waist. He came to Simon Peter, who said to him, "Master, are you going to wash my feet?" Jesus answered and said to him, "What I am doing, you do not understand now, but you will understand later." Peter said to him, "You will never wash my feet." Jesus answered him, "Unless I wash you, you will have no inheritance with me." Simon Peter said to him, "Master, then not only my feet, but my hands and head as well." Jesus said to him, "Whoever has bathed has no need except to have his feet washed, for he is clean all over; so you are clean, but not all." For he knew who would betray him; for this reason, he said, "Not all of you are clean."

So when he had washed their feet and put his garments back on and reclined at table again, he said to them, "Do you realize what I have done for you? You call me 'teacher' and 'master,' and rightly so, for indeed I am. If I, therefore, the master and teacher, have washed your feet, you ought to wash one another's feet. I have given you a model to follow, so that as I have done for you, you should also do."

Brief Silence

For Reflection

This sacred night, with its ritual of footwashing, is a profound reminder of what our Christian living is all about. Jesus invites each of us to be washed and, indeed, we have been washed in the waters of baptism. This plunges us deeply into Jesus' saving mystery. This demands of us that we, too, become servants to all. In this gospel Jesus shows us that love—sacrificing self unreservedly for the good of others—is down-to-earth practical.

Jesus raises humble service of others to a new level as a symbol of love. The simple gesture of Jesus in the gospel reminds us that love knows no bounds, excludes no one, is a remarkable gesture of self-sacrifice. Yes, Jesus loved us to the end. But the end isn't the cross. The end is the ongoing invitation to stand at the messianic table and be nourished by the Body and Blood of Christ. We come to the table worthily when we do as the Master has done: empty ourselves in self-sacrifice for the good of others.

✦ Footwashing is a metaphor for sacrificing for the good of others. This metaphor is made concrete in my ministry whenever I . . .

Brief Silence

Prayer

Gracious God, you teach us that humble service is an expression of our love for you and each other. Lead us more deeply into this love as we journey toward eternal life. We ask this through Christ our Lord. **Amen**.

At this time when we celebrate with joy the resurrection of Jesus from the dead, we also renew our baptismal promises. Let us renew this commitment to the risen Lord by surrendering ourselves to God's loving presence . . .

Prayer

God of new life, you raised Jesus from the dead as a sign of your love and our salvation. Hear our prayers so that we may be healed of anything that keeps us from sharing the joy of this new life. We ask this through Christ our Lord. **Amen**.

Gospel (Luke 24:1-12)

At daybreak on the first day of the week the women who had come from Galilee with Jesus took the spices they had prepared and went to the tomb. They found the stone rolled away from the tomb; but when they entered, they did not find the body of the Lord Jesus. While they were puzzling over this, behold, two men in dazzling garments appeared to them. They were terrified and bowed their faces to the ground. They said to them, "Why do you seek the living one among the dead? He is not here, but he has been raised. Remember what he said to you while he was still in Galilee, that the Son of Man must be handed over to sinners and be crucified, and rise on the third day." And they remembered his words. Then they returned from the tomb and announced all these things to the eleven and to all the others. The women were Mary Magdalene, Joanna, and Mary the mother of James; the others who accompanied them also told this to the apostles, but their story seemed like nonsense and they did not believe them. But Peter got up and ran to the tomb, bent down, and saw the burial cloths alone; then he went home amazed at what had happened.

Brief Silence

For Reflection

Even on this day when the gospel announces the risen Lord, we feel the contradictions that the resurrection mystery arouses—seeing and believing on the one hand, misunderstanding and confusion on the other. This mystery defies all human understanding. These Easter stories tell us that the resurrection isn't something we understand but believe and live. Instead of trying to understand, we simply "run" to the mystery and embrace it so that we, like John, can enter into it and see and believe. In John's gospel seeing and believing aren't mental exercises but actions that express one's inner disposition. Our belief in the resurrection is a matter of a willingness to embrace self-sacrifice, allowing others to "feast" on us.

The paradox of Christianity is that dying to self isn't something to avoid, but is the way we remove the stone that blocks our own hearts from receiving new life. We need only to take the time to contemplate this mystery and recognize the good with which God blesses us. We need to see beyond the obvious—an empty tomb and the demands of self-emptying—to the glory that God has bestowed through Christ Jesus.

✦ "Seeing" and "believing" in Jesus' resurrection means to me . . . The way I try to live this mystery is . . .

Brief Silence

Prayer

Glorious God of the living, you bestow grace beyond compare and life beyond measure. Be with us as we embrace this resurrection mystery and journey toward the fullness of life with you. We ask this through Christ our Lord. **Amen**.

Let us ask for deeper faith in the risen Lord, so that we may exclaim with full hearts, "My Lord and my God!" . . .

Prayer

Heavenly Father, your Son appeared to the disciples and breathed on them the Holy Spirit. With the help of that same Spirit may we believe with all our hearts and serve others with all our wills. We ask this through Christ our Lord. **Amen**.

Gospel (John 20:19-31)

On the evening of that first day of the week, when the doors were locked, where the disciples were, for fear of the Jews, Jesus came and stood in their midst and said to them, "Peace be with you." When he had said this, he showed them his hands and his side. The disciples rejoiced when they saw the Lord. Jesus said to them again, "Peace be with you. As the Father has sent me, so I send you." And when he had said this, he breathed on them and said to them, "Receive the Holy Spirit. Whose sins you forgive are forgiven them, and whose sins you retain are retained."

Thomas, called Didymus, one of the Twelve, was not with them when Jesus came. So the other disciples said to him, "We have seen the Lord." But he said to them, "Unless I see the mark of the nails in his hands and put my finger into the nailmarks and put my hand into his side, I will not believe."

Now a week later his disciples were again inside and Thomas was with them. Jesus came, although the doors were locked, and stood in their midst and said, "Peace be with you." Then he said to Thomas, "Put your finger here and see my hands, and bring your hand and put it into my side, and do not be unbelieving, but believe." Thomas answered and said to him, "My Lord and my God!" Jesus said to him,

"Have you come to believe because you have seen me? Blessed are those who have not seen and have believed."

Now Jesus did many other signs in the presence of his disciples that are not written in this book. But these are written that you may come to believe that Jesus is the Christ, the Son of God, and that through this belief you may have life in his name.

Brief Silence

For Reflection

The risen Lord appears and three times he addresses the gathered disciples: "Peace be with you." What is this peace he brings? It is a peace that allays fears, empowers forgiveness, and prompts us to accept the reality of suffering and death as doorways to new life. The peace Jesus brings prompts us to face death rather than cower from it. The peace Jesus brings prompts us to set right our relationships. This peace is new life: the Spirit breathed into us by the risen Lord. This peace bestows on us the life and power of Jesus himself and with it we can make a difference in our world. The condition of this gift of peace, however, is belief. Belief is not merely an exercise in intellectual consent but a commitment of self to acceptance of the Life that is given us. We know *to whom and what* our belief is directed: to Jesus and the gift of new life. We know *how* we receive new life: through Jesus' gift of the breath of the Holy Spirit dwelling within us. We know the *fruit* of this new life: peace and forgiveness.

✦ Where God is calling me to receive the peace of the risen Lord is . . . to extend this peace is . . .

Brief Silence

Prayer

God of peace, your Spirit brings us unity and harmony. Open us to your gracious divine presence, transform us into peacemakers, and bring us to share in your eternal life. We ask this through Christ our Lord. **Amen**.

Even as we celebrate risen life, we are challenged to respond to Jesus in new ways and learn to love him ever more deeply. We pause to consider how we might do this in our ministry . . .

Prayer

Loving God, your Son gives us an abundance of food for our journey toward new life. Be with us as we strive to hear his call and respond to his commands. We ask this through Christ our Lord. **Amen**.

Gospel (John 21:1-14 [Longer Form: John 21:1-19])

At that time, Jesus revealed himself again to his disciples at the Sea of Tiberias. He revealed himself in this way. Together were Simon Peter, Thomas called Didymus, Nathanael from Cana in Galilee, Zebedee's sons, and two others of his disciples. Simon Peter said to them, "I am going fishing." They said to him, "We also will come with you." So they went out and got into the boat, but that night they caught nothing. When it was already dawn, Jesus was standing on the shore; but the disciples did not realize that it was Jesus. Jesus said to them, "Children, have you caught anything to eat?" They answered him, "No." So he said to them, "Cast the net over the right side of the boat and you will find something." So they cast it, and were not able to pull it in because of the number of fish. So the disciple whom Jesus loved said to Peter, "It is the Lord." When Simon Peter heard that it was the Lord, he tucked in his garment, for he was lightly clad, and jumped into the sea. The other disciples came in the boat, for they were not far from shore, only about a hundred yards, dragging the net with the fish. When they climbed out on shore, they saw a charcoal fire with fish on it and bread. Jesus said to them, "Bring some of the fish you just caught." So Simon Peter went over and dragged the net ashore full of one hundred fifty-three large fish. Even though there were so many, the net was not torn. Jesus said to them, "Come, have breakfast." And none of the disciples dared to ask him, "Who are you?" because they realized it was the Lord. Jesus came over and took the bread and gave it to them, and in like manner the fish. This was now the third time Jesus was revealed to his disciples after being raised from the dead.

Brief Silence

For Reflection

In this Sunday's gospel Jesus addresses the adult, capable fishermen disciples as "children." The appearance of the risen Jesus to them on the seashore is a presence bringing new life, challenging them to growth. Easter life is a constant invitation to growth, a constant opening to God's unexpected gifts of abundance, a constant invitation to faithful response, which in itself is growth leading to new life. These "children" disciples need yet to grow.

It would seem as though the disciples are still missing the point of the resurrection and how it changes one's life, because Peter and several other disciples revert to what is familiar—they go fishing. On their own they catch nothing. It is only in response to Jesus' command from the seashore that they cast their nets and pull in a great catch. Heeding Jesus' commands and sharing in risen life is the only way to grow in love. This means that our own love must be so great that we respond to Jesus and choose to follow him.

✦ The ways I feed and tend to God's flock (my family and my parish) are . . .

Brief Silence

Prayer

Shepherd God, you care for each of us with love and compassion. Be with us in all the frustrations of life, and help us to hear your commands to follow you more closely. We ask this through Christ our Lord. **Amen**.

We ask God to bless us and remind us of the care and concern God has for us. Let us open our hearts to the Good Shepherd and follow him more faithfully . . .

Prayer

Heavenly Father, you shepherd us and care for us with unsurpassed faithfulness. Keep us free from harm, heal us of all our anxieties, and help us to hear and respond to the call of your voice. We ask this through Christ our Lord. **Amen**.

Gospel (John 10:27-30)

Jesus said: "My sheep hear my voice; I know them, and they follow me. I give them eternal life, and they shall never perish. No one can take them out of my hand. My Father, who has given them to me, is greater than all, and no one can take them out of the Father's hand. The Father and I are one."

Brief Silence

For Reflection

The gospel conveys Jesus' great, tender care and concern for his "sheep." This care does not keep his followers from anxieties and cares. It does assure them of protection in the midst of persecution ("no one can take them out of my hand") and of eternal life ("they shall never perish"). But this assurance only comes when we followers of Jesus "hear [his] voice" and live out of the personal relationship God offers us.

By juxtaposing hearing and following, the gospel intimates that hearing Jesus is already following him. We follow first by listening. The call to follow is a call to faithful obedience (the root word for obedience means "to hear"). In other words, hearing Jesus—heeding his voice—is already an act of following. But probably most important, hearing Jesus' voice is already our participation in eternal life. Ultimately, this promise of eternal life is the reassurance and care that Jesus offers: by hearing Jesus' voice and following him we will not perish but already share in Jesus' eternal life. No better care than this could the Good Shepherd offer!

✦ My manner of distributing Holy Communion helps others experience the care and concern of the Good Shepherd when . . .

Brief Silence

Prayer

Good and gentle Shepherd, you reassure us of your care and protection. Hear our pleas for guidance and help, that one day we may rest with you in eternal life. We ask this through Christ our Lord. **Amen**.

We pause to reflect and pray about the full measure of love and life God gives us. May we grow in our own self-giving love for which Jesus is the model . . .

Prayer

Bountiful God, you have shown us the depth of your love in the dying and rising of Jesus. May we enter into that mystery more fully during this Easter time, and learn to love you and each other more perfectly. We ask this through Christ our Lord. **Amen**.

Gospel (John 13:31-33a, 34-35)

When Judas had left them, Jesus said, "Now is the Son of Man glorified, and God is glorified in him. If God is glorified in him, God will also glorify him in himself, and God will glorify him at once. My children, I will be with you only a little while longer. I give you a new commandment: love one another. As I have loved you, so you also should love one another. This is how all will know that you are my disciples, if you have love for one another."

Brief Silence

For Reflection

The "new commandment" that Jesus gives is not simply to "love" but to love *as he has loved us*. With respect to loving, "how far" is the question. Jesus' commandment to love requires a new way of living: regard for others without counting the cost to ourselves. Jesus' death simultaneously reveals the full measure of his love and his glory. Our death—dying to self—reveals the full measure of our love for others and leads to a share in Jesus' glory. Love is the doorway to glory.

Jesus doesn't ask of us anything that he himself hasn't already done to the fullest: the Good Friday–Easter events make clear the extent of Jesus' love for us—he will lay down his very life so that we may have a share in his risen life. As disciples we are commanded to love as the Master loved; if our love is to imitate his, then our love must also include the willingness to lay down our lives for others. The kind of love that Jesus commands leads to self-emptying dying to self. It is the way to new life. Loving one another must be the very way we live.

✦ Distributing Holy Communion extends the full measure of God's love in these ways . . .

Brief Silence

Prayer

God our Lover, you hold us intimately in the palm of your hand. Help us to love one another as you have loved us, and prepare us one day to be with you forever in heaven. We ask this through Christ our Lord. **Amen**.

We pause to ask God's help to keep Jesus' word faithfully, and to live in peace with unafraid and untroubled hearts . . .

Prayer

All-knowing God, you send your Holy Spirit to teach us all things. Help us to be faithful to the indwelling of your grace within us, and to spread the Good News of your peace and love. We ask this through Christ our Lord. **Amen**.

Gospel **(John 14:23-29)**

Jesus said to his disciples: "Whoever loves me will keep my word, and my Father will love him, and we will come to him and make our dwelling with him. Whoever does not love me does not keep my words; yet the word you hear is not mine but that of the Father who sent me.

"I have told you this while I am with you. The Advocate, the Holy Spirit, whom the Father will send in my name, will teach you everything and remind you of all that I told you. Peace I leave with you; my peace I give to you. Not as the world gives do I give it to you. Do not let your hearts be troubled or afraid. You heard me tell you, 'I am going away and I will come back to you.' If you loved me, you would rejoice that I am going to the Father; for the Father is greater than I. And now I have told you this before it happens, so that when it happens you may believe."

Brief Silence

For Reflection

It seems hard enough for most of us to have the integrity to keep our own word and promises faithfully. Lo and behold, in this gospel Jesus takes this one step further: "Whoever loves me will keep *my* word . . ." In last Sunday's gospel Jesus admonished us to love not on our own terms but as he loves. This week he commands us to keep not our word but his word. If we have difficulty keeping our own word (and, realistically, sometimes we do), how in the world can we be successful in keeping *Jesus*' word? Besides, Jesus' word is much more than simply what Jesus said and taught. It is the way he lived. Jesus' words and deeds coalesce into the same reality, that is, a life of self-giving that brings salvation. Our Christian understanding of love rests precisely in the breadth of self-giving we are willing to offer. Keeping Jesus' word ultimately means that we make all of the gospel our own. This is surely no small task! But the rewards are not small either: God's indwelling that brings us new life.

✦ This Easter, the word of Jesus that I am being called to keep by living it is . . .

Brief Silence

Prayer

God of joy, your word is made visible in the good you bring us. Help us to ponder Scripture lovingly and to live your word fervently. We ask this through Christ our Lord. **Amen**.

We pause to call to mind our baptism, through which we receive the Holy Spirit, God's divine indwelling. Let us open ourselves to God's presence so that we can be this presence for others . . .

Prayer

Dear Father of us all, your Son ascended into heaven to take his place at your right hand in glory. Help us to be faithful to his command to spread the Gospel to all nations, and to be his risen presence for everyone we meet. We ask this through Christ our Lord. **Amen**.

Gospel (Luke 24:46-53)

Jesus said to his disciples: "Thus it is written that the Christ would suffer and rise from the dead on the third day and that repentance, for the forgiveness of sins, would be preached in his name to all the nations, beginning from Jerusalem. You are witnesses of these things. And behold I am sending the promise of my Father upon you; but stay in the city until you are clothed with power from on high."

Then he led them out as far as Bethany, raised his hands, and blessed them. As he blessed them he parted from them and was taken up to heaven. They did him homage and then returned to Jerusalem with great joy, and they were continually in the temple praising God.

Brief Silence

For Reflection

Jesus' disappearance from sight does not mark an absence, but a new kind of presence. In the "absence" left by his ascension, we his followers are commissioned to "preach[ ] in his name to all the nations." What is it we preach? That suffering and even death lead to new life and that forgiveness will be granted to all who repent. His very ascension into heaven is our commissioning on earth because, "clothed with power from on high," we are now the visible presence of Jesus.

His absence brings a presence—the Holy Spirit who is the "power from on high" with which we are consecrated to continue Jesus' saving mission. We don't do this on our own, as Jesus promised. We can't set out to take up Jesus' mission to preach the Good News until we receive the Holy Spirit. This ensures us that our work isn't ours but Christ's. Ultimately, our mission is to preach not simply events but a Person—Jesus Christ, the risen One. Even more, with the Spirit, we *are* the presence of the risen Lord.

✦ I distribute the presence of Jesus in Holy Communion. My daily living distributes the presence of Jesus in that . . .

Brief Silence

Prayer

Ever-present God, you never leave us orphans, but always are with us through each other. May we be open to your Spirit's presence within us and one day come to share everlasting life with you in heaven. We ask this through Christ our Lord. **Amen**.

We pause during our busy lives to remember with grateful hearts Jesus' intimate love for us. Let us open ourselves to God's loving presence . . .

Prayer

Holy and righteous Father, you have sent your Son to make known to us your love and will for us. Remain in us, that we may be faithful to the mission your Son has given to us to make known the Good News of salvation. We ask this through Christ our Lord. **Amen**.

Gospel (John 17:20-26)

Lifting up his eyes to heaven, Jesus prayed, saying: "Holy Father, I pray not only for them, but also for those who will believe in me through their word, so that they may all be one, as you, Father, are in me and I in you, that they also may be in us, that the world may believe that you sent me. And I have given them the glory you gave me, so that they may be one, as we are one, I in them and you in me, that they may be brought to perfection as one, that the world may know that you sent me, and that you loved them even as you loved me. Father, they are your gift to me. I wish that where I am they also may be with me, that they may see my glory that you gave me, because you loved me before the foundation of the world. Righteous Father, the world also does not know you, but I know you, and they know that you sent me. I made known to them your name and I will make it known, that the love with which you loved me may be in them and I in them."

Brief Silence

For Reflection

Prayer reveals the deepest desire of our hearts and our truest selves. As Jesus prays in this gospel, we learn what is deepest in his heart. What is more, Jesus' prayer teaches us that in the unity we share as the one Body of Christ, we already participate in Jesus' glory. By being the one Body of Christ, we share in his identity, and so also are already united with the Trinity in all its glory. Jesus' prayer reminds us that being a disciple means that we already share in Jesus' glory. We are the Father's gift to Jesus, we are intimately loved into a union with God and each other, and we already share in divine glory.

In this intimate prayer of Jesus before his suffering and death, we see clearly how much Jesus sustains us in our discipleship. Our peek into what is deepest in Jesus' heart encourages us. The gift of the Spirit that we receive helps us see who we are to be as the one Body of Christ: those whose lives are spent in self-sacrificing surrender for the sake of others. Our glory lies in imitating Jesus, knowing that dying to self leads to risen life.

✦ "I pray . . . that they may all be one." I seek to bring about communion in my daily living when . . .

Brief Silence

Prayer

O God, you wish us to know and love you with all our hearts. Be with us as we strive in our everyday lives to be faithful to your presence, that one day we may enjoy everlasting glory with you. We ask this through Christ our Lord. **Amen**.

On this Pentecost Sunday we celebrate the gift of the Holy Spirit. We once again ask God to remind us that divine life dwells within us and we must always be faithful to the gift we have been given . . .

Prayer

Our Father in heaven, you send your Spirit upon us to be with us always. May the Spirit teach us to love more deeply, keep your word perseveringly, and bring us to everlasting life. We ask this through Christ our Lord. **Amen**.

Gospel (John 14:15-16, 23b-26 [or: John 20:19-23])

Jesus said to his disciples: "If you love me, you will keep my commandments. And I will ask the Father, and he will give you another Advocate to be with you always.

"Whoever loves me will keep my word, and my Father will love him, and we will come to him and make our dwelling with him. Those who do not love me do not keep my words; yet the word you hear is not mine but that of the Father who sent me.

"I have told you this while I am with you. The Advocate, the Holy Spirit whom the Father will send in my name, will teach you everything and remind you of all that I told you."

Brief Silence

For Reflection

With the sending of the Holy Spirit who is "another Advocate," we followers of Jesus are never bereft of divine presence. This new Advocate teaches us just as Jesus taught the first disciples. This new Advocate "calls" (Latin, *advocare* = to call) us to faithful discipleship and "supports" (Greek, *paráklētos* = helper) us in our efforts to love Jesus. This new Advocate enables us to love and live as Jesus did, continuing his saving mission and making him present through us.

God can give us no greater gift than a share in the very life of God's divine presence. This is what we celebrate on this solemnity of Pentecost—God dwells within us, giving us a share in divine life. Moreover, since we all share in the same life, the Spirit is the bond of unity among us. Pentecost is a celebration of both the gift of the Spirit and the effects of that gift—we are sharers in the one Body of Christ who take up Jesus' mission to preach the Good News of salvation.

✦ In receiving the Spirit I become an advocate of God's presence. This requires that I . . .

Brief Silence

Prayer

God of Spirit and truth, you dwell within us and call us to salvation. Be with us as we strive to be faithful to you and bring us one day to enjoy an everlasting dwelling place with you. We ask this through Christ our Lord. **Amen**.

This Sunday when we celebrate the glory of our triune God, we also celebrate that God dwells within and among us. Let us open ourselves to this mystery of divine presence . . .

Prayer

God of truth and glory, the mystery of your three Persons is revealed to us by your constant love. Help us to increase your love within us, that we may love each other more deeply. We ask this through Christ our Lord. **Amen**.

Gospel (John 16:12-15)

Jesus said to his disciples: "I have much more to tell you, but you cannot bear it now. But when he comes, the Spirit of truth, he will guide you to all truth. He will not speak on his own, but he will speak what he hears, and will declare to you the things that are coming. He will glorify me, because he will take from what is mine and declare it to you. Everything that the Father has is mine; for this reason I told you that he will take from what is mine and declare it to you."

Brief Silence

For Reflection

Surely this mystery of our God is so great that we "cannot bear it now" fully. Revelation is always gradual. The fullness of "all truth" would be overwhelming if we heard it in its full power, for the ultimate revelation—"all truth"—is the gift of the Trinity itself dwelling within and among us. As we faithfully live Jesus' command to make known the Good News, we gradually become aware that no one of us can reveal God, but together, in community, we are that presence. The stronger the community in openness to encountering God, the more clear to us is the revelation of divine presence. We gradually learn from each other how much God loves us by the divine presence that we encounter and mediate for each other.

The majesty of the Trinity defies any intellectual unraveling of the mystery. An intellectual exercise is not what God reveals to us nor asks of us. God gives triune self to us simply so that we can encounter God's glory and share among us the grace, peace, and hope of divine presence.

✦ I carry out my ministry in a way that reveals both God's majesty and God's intimacy among us by . . .

Brief Silence

Prayer

O God, you have claimed us as your own. Nurture us, strengthen us, bring us to unity so that we may shine forth your glory and presence. We ask this through Christ our Lord. **Amen**.

We celebrate God's gracious gift of abundance to us in the gift of Christ's Body and Blood for our nourishment. Let us open ourselves to this great mystery and prepare to receive this abundance from our God . . .

Prayer

Bountiful God who reigns with justice and mercy, you feed us with Bread from heaven. May we be satisfied fully only by you, and raise grateful hearts to you for the gift of Eucharist. We ask this through Christ our Lord. **Amen**.

Gospel **(Luke 9:11b-17)**

Jesus spoke to the crowds about the kingdom of God, and he healed those who needed to be cured. As the day was drawing to a close, the Twelve approached him and said, "Dismiss the crowd so that they can go to the surrounding villages and farms and find lodging and provisions; for we are in a deserted place here." He said to them, "Give them some food yourselves." They replied, "Five loaves and two fish are all we have, unless we ourselves go and buy food for all these people." Now the men there numbered about five thousand. Then he said to his disciples, "Have them sit down in groups of about fifty." They did so and made them all sit down. Then taking the five loaves and the two fish, and look-ing up to heaven, he said the blessing over them, broke them, and gave them to the disciples to set before the crowd. They all ate and were satisfied. And when the leftover fragments were picked up, they filled twelve wicker baskets.

Brief Silence

For Reflection

Jesus' gospel command is clear: we are to feed others. We give to others not from the "deserted place" of our own hearts but from the "leftover fragments" of God's blessings. God's abundant nourishment is most startlingly given in the handing over of Jesus' life—on the cross, in the Bread and Wine. As Jesus' followers we are to be God's abundant nourishment for others by our own self-gift of life. God's abundant giving continues in our own self-giving lives.

The Twelve apparently still haven't quite gotten this message of abundance and self-giving. They approach Jesus with the instruction to "dismiss the crowd"; this is clearly a practical response to a practical situation—a hungry, tired, large crowd. Jesus' response makes clear God's intention for us: "Give them some food yourselves." Perhaps the amazement of this gospel and festival is that God so willingly chooses us humans to make known divine superabundance and blessing. We are invited to participate in God's graciousness by our passing on of this abundance. Our lives, then, must witness to the intersection of need and generosity. Our own self-gift makes present divine generosity.

✦ My ministry of distributing Holy Communion at Mass urges me to distribute myself to those in need by . . .

Brief Silence

Prayer

Generous God of abundance, you give us all good things beyond compare. Be with us as we struggle to give to others out of our own abundance. We ask this through Christ our Lord. **Amen**.

In the gospel we hear the story of the repentant woman who washes Jesus' feet with her tears. Let us pause for time in prayer to open ourselves to the God who washes away our sins . . .

Prayer

Tolerant God, you are patient as we learn your ways of forgiveness and mercy. May we come to you in love and humility, that you may heal us of our weaknesses. We ask this through Christ our Lord. **Amen**.

Gospel (Luke 7:36-50 [Longer Form: Luke 7:36–8:3])

A Pharisee invited Jesus to dine with him, and he entered the Pharisee's house and reclined at table. Now there was a sinful woman in the city who learned that he was at table in the house of the Pharisee. Bringing an alabaster flask of ointment, she stood behind him at his feet weeping and began to bathe his feet with her tears. Then she wiped them with her hair, kissed them, and anointed them with the ointment. When the Pharisee who had invited him saw this he said to himself, "If this man were a prophet, he would know who and what sort of woman this is who is touching him, that she is a sinner." Jesus said to him in reply, "Simon, I have something to say to you." "Tell me, teacher," he said. "Two people were in debt to a certain creditor; one owed five hundred days' wages and the other owed fifty. Since they were unable to repay the debt, he forgave it for both. Which of them will love him more?" Simon said in reply, "The one, I suppose, whose larger debt was forgiven." He said to him, "You have judged rightly." Then he turned to the woman and said to Simon, "Do you see this woman? When I entered your house, you did not give me water for my feet, but she has bathed them with her tears and wiped them with her hair. You did not give me a kiss, but she has not ceased kissing my feet since the time I entered. You did not anoint my head with oil, but she anointed my feet with ointment. So I tell you, her many sins have been forgiven because she has shown great love. But the one to whom little is forgiven, loves little." He said to her, "Your sins are forgiven." The others at table said to themselves, "Who is this who even forgives sins?" But he said to the woman, "Your faith has saved you; go in peace."

Brief Silence

For Reflection

Jesus asks, "Do you see this woman?" The Pharisee looks at her and sees only a sinner. Jesus looks at her and sees a sinner who repents. He sees her tremendous humility, her great sorrow, her desire to minister to him in his need, her "great love," her saving faith. The woman sees Jesus as One whom she can love and who loves her in return. This relationship brings her salvation and peace. Jesus is able to do for the sinful woman what he might have done for the Pharisee, who only needed to truly encounter Jesus for who he is.

While the woman and her actions seem to be the centerpiece of this gospel, what is really central is openness to others, accepting them for who they are, and seeing rightly into our own hearts before we judge the heart of another. Jesus is the model for seeing rightly. What does Jesus see when he looks at us? What do we see when we look at one another?

✦ My manner of distributing Holy Communion lets others see in me . . . I see in them . . .

Brief Silence

Prayer

O Lord, may we see as only you can see into our hearts! Help us to come to you in humility and love, that one day we may kneel before you in everlasting glory. We ask this through Christ our Lord. **Amen**.

Jesus invites us to follow him, but he also tells us that discipleship has its cost: we must deny ourselves and take up our cross daily. Let us ask God in prayer to strengthen us on our Christian journey . . .

Prayer

God of life, your Son Jesus asks us to take up our cross daily and follow him. May we know that whatever cross we bear, you are always there to strengthen and uphold us. We ask this through Christ our Lord. **Amen**.

Gospel **(Luke 9:18-24)**

Once when Jesus was praying in solitude, and the disciples were with him, he asked them, "Who do the crowds say that I am?" They said in reply, "John the Baptist; others, Elijah; still others, 'One of the ancient prophets has arisen.'" Then he said to them, "But who do you say that I am?" Peter said in reply, "The Christ of God." He rebuked them and directed them not to tell this to anyone.

He said, "The Son of Man must suffer greatly and be rejected by the elders, the chief priests, and the scribes, and be killed and on the third day be raised."

Then he said to all, "If anyone wishes to come after me, he must deny himself and take up his cross daily and follow me. For whoever wishes to save his life will lose it, but whoever loses his life for my sake will save it."

Brief Silence

For Reflection

Jesus asks again a pretty simple question about his identity. Now Peter answers, but a surprise lies in how Jesus clarifies the meaning of "the Christ." He is to "suffer greatly," "be rejected," "be killed." This is the way Jesus becomes who he really is—the risen One. To realize our own truest identity, we must daily die to ourselves. This is the way we become who we truly are to be— followers of Jesus who daily die to ourselves and daily share more and more in the life of the risen Lord.

Jesus is so much in touch with his ultimate *mission*—to "suffer greatly," "be rejected," "be killed," and "be raised"—that he actually defines his identity in terms of it. His mission is an extension of who Jesus is—Savior. We usually think of Jesus' mission as teaching and preaching, healing and working miracles, and so it was. But underlying these activities is the ultimate one—his suffering, death, and resurrection. So it is with us.

✦ We recognize Jesus in his Body and Blood. The way I recognize Jesus in denying self and taking up my cross is . . .

Brief Silence

Prayer

Saving God, you never ask us to bear a cross heavier than we can carry. Be with us as we journey in your Son's saving ways, and welcome us one day into your everlasting glory. We ask this through Christ our Lord. **Amen**.

This Sunday's gospel challenges us to follow Jesus on his journey to Jerusalem, where he will suffer, die, and be raised to new life. Let us prepare ourselves to hear this call and answer resolutely . . .

Prayer

Loving God, our Savior your Son set his course for Jerusalem, where his final glory would be shown. Help us to follow him faithfully and resolutely, never wavering when discouraged or distressed, for you are always with us. We ask this through Christ our Lord. **Amen**.

Gospel (Luke 9:51-62)

When the days for Jesus' being taken up were fulfilled, he resolutely determined to journey to Jerusalem, and he sent messengers ahead of him. On the way they entered a Samaritan village to prepare for his reception there, but they would not welcome him because the destination of his journey was Jerusalem. When the disciples James and John saw this they asked, "Lord, do you want us to call down fire from heaven to consume them?" Jesus turned and rebuked them, and they journeyed to another village.

As they were proceeding on their journey someone said to him, "I will follow you wherever you go." Jesus answered him, "Foxes have dens and birds of the sky have nests, but the Son of Man has nowhere to rest his head."

And to another he said, "Follow me." But he replied, "Lord, let me go first and bury my father." But he answered him, "Let the dead bury their dead. But you, go and proclaim the kingdom of God." And another said, "I will follow you, Lord, but first let me say farewell to my family at home." To him Jesus said, "No one who sets a hand to the plow and looks to what was left behind is fit for the kingdom of God."

Brief Silence

For Reflection

This gospel depicts various responses to and interactions with Jesus: some refuse him entrance into their village, some naively swear to follow wherever he leads, some put the exigencies of life ahead of following him. Each response suggests that people have some sense of what the cost of following Jesus is. Throughout, Jesus consistently indicates that those who follow him must separate themselves from anything that hinders their resolutely journeying with him through death to new life. The price is high, but so are the stakes and so is the reward.

We must be as resolutely determined to accept the dying to self that is necessary to follow Jesus and to cooperate with him in establishing God's reign as Jesus was resolutely determined to go to his own suffering and death. We can be neither naive nor self-excusing. To be "fit for the kingdom of God," we must keep our eyes on Jesus and our destiny. We must let him be our motivation to stay the course. The course: Jerusalem. The price: dying. The stakes: new life. This is surely all the motivation we could possibly need: following Jesus brings new life.

✦ The way even the eucharistic banquet directs me toward Jerusalem is . . .

Brief Silence

Prayer

God of life, you call us to Jerusalem and the new life that is ours when we are faithful to dying to self. May we never hesitate on our journey, beckoned by the eternal life that awaits all Jesus' faithful followers. We ask this through Christ our Lord. **Amen**.

In this gospel Jesus sends forth the seventy-two disciples to minister in his name and reap the abundant harvest of the presence of the kingdom of God. May we hear Jesus' call and open ourselves to God's presence and mercy . . .

Prayer

Lord God of creation, you call us to be laborers for your harvest. May we respond to your call faithfully and labor fruitfully so your peace will reign in our hearts. We ask this through Christ our Lord. **Amen**.

Gospel (Luke 10:1-9 [Longer Form: Luke 10:1-12, 17-20])

At that time the Lord appointed seventy-two others whom he sent ahead of him in pairs to every town and place he intended to visit. He said to them, "The harvest is abundant but the laborers are few; so ask the master of the harvest to send out laborers for his harvest. Go on your way; behold, I am sending you like lambs among wolves. Carry no money bag, no sack, no sandals; and greet no one along the way. Into whatever house you enter, first say, 'Peace to this household.' If a peaceful person lives there, your peace will rest on him; but if not, it will return to you. Stay in the same house and eat and drink what is offered to you, for the laborer deserves his payment. Do not move about from one house to another. Whatever town you enter and they welcome you, eat what is set before you, cure the sick in it and say to them, 'The kingdom of God is at hand for you.'"

Brief Silence

For Reflection

In this Sunday's gospel Jesus refers three times to an abundant harvest. The nature of this harvest is evident through the ministry of the disciples Jesus sends forth: peace, stability, nourishment, healing, rejoicing. This is no ordinary harvest of the fruits of the earth. This harvest is the fruit of God's kingdom "at hand" through the very ministry of Jesus and his disciples. Moreover, the harvest is being reaped today through us who continue to go forth in Jesus' name.

Note that some of the abundant harvest goes to the laborer-disciples who are sent forth: they have the power to heal, are nourished, are welcomed, cast out demons, and rejoice. Some of the abundant harvest goes to those who receive the ministry: peace and healing. The abundant harvest of both laborers and recipients is a sign of God's presence. And where God is present, there is God's kingdom. Rather than being measured by spacious skies, prairies of ripe wheat, majestic mountains, sobering deserts, rivers and lakes replete with commerce, God's kingdom is measured by the abundance of goodness, care for others, growth toward new life.

✦ I have experienced the abundance of the eucharistic banquet when . . . I extend it toward others when . . .

Brief Silence

Prayer

O good God, your kingdom is present wherever people labor in peace and justice. Help us to be faithful laborers, that one day we may enjoy the harvest of eternal life with you. We ask this through Christ our Lord. **Amen**.

The passage about the Good Samaritan is a familiar parable reminding us to love and care for each other. May we open ourselves during this prayer to God's love and care for us . . .

Prayer

Good and loving God, you care for us beyond our understanding, and love us with unbounded hospitality. May we look upon all others as our neighbors, extending to them your care and love. We ask this through Christ our Lord. **Amen**.

Gospel (Luke 10:25-37)

There was a scholar of the law who stood up to test Jesus and said, "Teacher, what must I do to inherit eternal life?" Jesus said to him, "What is written in the law? How do you read it?" He said in reply, *"You shall love the Lord, your God, with all your heart, with all your being, with all your strength, and with all your mind, and your neighbor as yourself."* He replied to him, "You have answered correctly; do this and you will live."

But because he wished to justify himself, he said to Jesus, "And who is my neighbor?" Jesus replied, "A man fell victim to robbers as he went down from Jerusalem to Jericho. They stripped and beat him and went off leaving him half-dead. A priest happened to be going down that road, but when he saw him, he passed by on the opposite side. Likewise a Levite came to the place, and when he saw him, he passed by on the opposite side. But a Samaritan traveler who came upon him was moved with compassion at the sight. He approached the victim, poured oil and wine over his wounds and bandaged them. Then he lifted him up on his own animal, took him to an inn, and cared for him. The next day he took out two silver coins and gave them to the innkeeper with the instruction, 'Take care of him. If you spend more than what I have given you, I shall repay you on my way back.' Which of these three, in your opinion, was neighbor to the robbers' victim?" He answered, "The one who treated him with mercy." Jesus said to him, "Go and do likewise."

Brief Silence

For Reflection

The lawyer puts an important question to Jesus, but an insincere one because he was really posing the question "to test" him. Jesus takes his question at face value and gives a right and all-embracing answer about how we "inherit eternal life." We must make love of God and neighbor the guiding focus of our lives here and now. The Good Samaritan parable admirably and clearly illustrates this kind of love. Our challenge: to go *this far* in our loving. "This far" has no limits, as Jesus himself illustrated by his own life. He went so far as even dying for us out of love. Our own loving one another must go this far, too. This kind of boundless love redefines who our neighbors are (everyone in need) and sets no limits on our time or care for others. Further, we show our love for God "with all [our] heart[s]" precisely when we love our neighbor "this far." Only by going "this far" can love truly become the guiding force in our lives. Only by going "this far" can we, like God, be defined as love.

✦ In loving God, I have gone this far . . . In loving my neighbor, I have gone this far . . . In my ministry, I have gone this far . . .

Brief Silence

Prayer

Merciful God, you show us how to care for each other by the care you give us. May we receive the life you offer us, and one day enter into eternal life. We ask this through Christ our Lord. **Amen**.

In this Sunday's gospel, Mary is busy listening to Jesus, while Martha remains busy serving him. Let us open our hearts to listen to God's word and to serve God by our obedience to that word . . .

Prayer

Teacher God, you remind us that we do well to listen to you and live your word. Help us to set our priorities so that you are always the center of our lives. We ask this through Christ our Lord. **Amen**.

Gospel (Luke 10:38-42)

Jesus entered a village where a woman whose name was Martha welcomed him. She had a sister named Mary who sat beside the Lord at his feet listening to him speak. Martha, burdened with much serving, came to him and said, "Lord, do you not care that my sister has left me by myself to do the serving? Tell her to help me." The Lord said to her in reply, "Martha, Martha, you are anxious and worried about many things. There is need of only one thing. Mary has chosen the better part and it will not be taken from her."

Brief Silence

For Reflection

What is each of the people in the gospel story doing? Martha is serving; Mary is listening; Jesus is teaching. While Jesus says that Mary has the "better part," this doesn't necessarily mean that listening to Jesus is either the only or the easier part. Listening to Jesus with a heart truly able to hear is difficult, indeed. Listening to Jesus is only the "better part" when it leads us to serve and teach as Jesus himself did. The effectiveness of our serving (and teaching, being disciples, caring for others, fulfilling our daily duties) is determined by the way we listen—to others, to Jesus through others.

A welcoming hospitality implies an "at-homeness" and belonging that parallels the unique relationship of disciple to Master. This kind of discipleship hospitality always brings new life. The "better part" Jesus promises is not just listening and being a disciple, but it is also sharing the new life that Jesus offers with others. Discipleship and listening cannot be separated. Neither can listening and serving.

✦ At Eucharist Christ is the Host, Guest, and Food. I go to the Host anticipating . . . I prepare for the Guest by . . . The Food nourishes me for . . .

Brief Silence

Prayer

Gracious God, you nourish us abundantly with new life. Open us to your presence, prepare us to serve others well, and help us journey steadfastly toward life everlasting. We ask this through Christ our Lord. **Amen**.

The disciples ask Jesus to teach them to pray. Let us surrender ourselves to God so that we can truly pray and open our hearts to a God who gives us all good things . . .

Prayer

Our Father, may your name be praised from sunrise to sunset. Pour forth your Spirit upon us so that we may wisely teach others of your goodness. We ask this through Christ our Lord. **Amen**.

Gospel (Luke 11:1-13)

Jesus was praying in a certain place, and when he had finished, one of his disciples said to him, "Lord, teach us to pray just as John taught his disciples." He said to them, "When you pray, say: / Father, hallowed be your name, / your kingdom come. / Give us each day our daily bread / and forgive us our sins / for we ourselves forgive everyone in debt to us, / and do not subject us to the final test."

And he said to them, "Suppose one of you has a friend to whom he goes at midnight and says, 'Friend, lend me three loaves of bread, for a friend of mine has arrived at my house from a journey and I have nothing to offer him,' and he says in reply from within, 'Do not bother me; the door has already been locked and my children and I are already in bed. I cannot get up to give you anything.' I tell you, if he does not get up to give the visitor the loaves because of their friendship, he will get up to give him whatever he needs because of his persistence.

"And I tell you, ask and you will receive; seek and you will find; knock and the door will be opened to you. For everyone who asks, receives; and the one who seeks, finds; and to the one who knocks, the door will be opened. What father among you would hand his son a snake when he asks for a fish? Or hand him a scorpion when he asks for an egg? If you then, who are wicked, know how to give good gifts to your children, how much more will the Father in heaven give the Holy Spirit to those who ask him?"

Brief Silence

For Reflection

In this gospel Jesus teaches us to whom we pray: God who is a generous and caring Father. He also teaches us for what we should pray: not just for immediate needs ("daily bread") but, more important, for ultimate needs—the furthering of God's kingdom, the gift of forgiveness, and protection from anything that would take us from God. It is persistence in prayer that brings us deeper into our relationship with God and opens us to receive these "good gifts" that God offers us. It is persistence in prayer that establishes and maintains the kind of relationship with God that assures us of the ultimate goal of life: eternal happiness with our divine Lover.

Jesus teaches us that the One to whom we pray is our "Father," whose love and care for us is unlimited. This deeply intimate and personal relationship with God inspires in us the confidence ("how much more . . .") to pray with "persistence," and the realization that what we pray for is not so important as the fact that we address God in such intimate terms. The prayer always deepens our relationship with God and this is already an answer to what we need.

◆ The ways I give "daily bread" to my family, neighbors, co-workers, those who are infirm, etc. are . . .

Brief Silence

Prayer

Our Father in heaven, you give us all good things and nourish us with Bread from heaven. Teach us to pray more fervently, that our whole lives are turned ever toward you. We ask this through Christ our Lord. **Amen**.

In this Sunday's gospel Jesus challenges us to focus on what matters to God. We place ourselves in God's presence and open ourselves to the fullness of life God wishes for us . . .

Prayer

O God who judges wisely and justly, you teach us to rely trustingly on your Divine Providence. Help us to be less concerned about storing up the wealth of this world and more concerned about the gifts only you can give. We ask this through Christ our Lord. **Amen**.

Gospel (Luke 12:13-21)

Someone in the crowd said to Jesus, "Teacher, tell my brother to share the inheritance with me." He replied to him, "Friend, who appointed me as your judge and arbitrator?" Then he said to the crowd, "Take care to guard against all greed, for though one may be rich, one's life does not consist of possessions."

Then he told them a parable. "There was a rich man whose land produced a bountiful harvest. He asked himself, 'What shall I do, for I do not have space to store my harvest?' And he said, 'This is what I shall do: I shall tear down my barns and build larger ones. There I shall store all my grain and other goods and I shall say to myself, "Now as for you, you have so many good things stored up for many years, rest, eat, drink, be merry!"' But God said to him, 'You fool, this night your life will be demanded of you; and the things you have prepared, to whom will they belong?' Thus will it be for all who store up treasure for themselves but are not rich in what matters to God."

Brief Silence

For Reflection

The rich man is a fool because he mistakenly thinks his future happiness is guaranteed by his possessions. Even had his life not been demanded of him, those possessions could not have bought him happiness. Jesus cautions us to "guard against" such greed and turn our attention to where our real inheritance lies: in the fullness of life God wishes to give us. How mistaken the rich man was to identify good living with material things and miss "what matters to God"!

We work hard for what we think is important to us, but we may end up with nothing because we have missed the whole point: life. Both the first reading and gospel speak of inheritance this Sunday; what we struggle all our lives to learn is that life does not consist of possessions nor our perceived security. Our true inheritance is not more possessions nor more security, but life with God. The only security we truly possess is a loving relationship with God—and this is surely what matters most to God. It should matter most to us.

✦ The way I distribute Holy Communion helps others see the fullness of life that God wishes for them by . . .

Brief Silence

Prayer

Saving God, what matters most to you is that we have eternal life with you. Turn us away from concerns about possessions and more perfectly toward what deepens our relationship with you and each other. We ask this through Christ our Lord. **Amen**.

This gospel reminds us that we are to be faithful servants of the Lord Jesus. We take time to open ourselves to God's presence and help . . .

Prayer

God who is Master of all the earth, you wish that we are vigilant for the many ways you come to us. Help us to be prepared to welcome you with open hearts. We ask this through Christ our Lord. **Amen**.

Gospel (Luke 12:35-40 [Longer Form: Luke 12:32-48])

Jesus said to his disciples: "Gird your loins and light your lamps and be like servants who await their master's return from a wedding, ready to open immediately when he comes and knocks. Blessed are those servants whom the master finds vigilant on his arrival. Amen, I say to you, he will gird himself, have them recline at table, and proceed to wait on them. And should he come in the second or third watch and find them prepared in this way, blessed are those servants. Be sure of this: if the master of the house had known the hour when the thief was coming, he would not have let his house be broken into. You also must be prepared, for at an hour you do not expect, the Son of Man will come."

Brief Silence

For Reflection

Jesus makes clear that the blessed servant is the one who does the master's will even when the master is absent. Being prepared for the master's presence is not a matter of calculating time; it is a matter of faithfulness. In the master's absence, the faithful servant acts as the master himself would—caring for others, giving them all they need. Doing the master's will and remaining faithful is *being* the master in his absence. Of such is discipleship.

What Jesus intimates in the parable is that we followers are being vigilant for the *master*, that is, Jesus himself, and our vigilance is expressed in doing as our Master would do. To have our hearts where our treasure is means to "act in accord with [Jesus'] will." This is our ultimate treasure: to give up our own wills and conform them to Jesus. This is our ultimate blessedness: to act responsibly, to treat others with dignity and care, to live righteously and faithfully.

✦ My ministry witnesses to my faithfulness to the Master when . . .

Brief Silence

Prayer

Faithful God, you desire that we act in accord with your will. Help us to do good, to avoid evil, and to ready ourselves to be welcomed into eternal life. We ask this through Christ our Lord. **Amen**.

On this day we celebrate the assumption of Mary into heaven. The promise of God's divine mercy is fulfilled as Mary joins her divine Son in everlasting glory. Let us pause to pray and ask God's help in being faithful as Mary was faithful . . .

Prayer

Gracious God, you brought Mary, body and soul, into heaven to dwell in your glory forever. May our whole being proclaim your presence, as did Mary, and remain always faithful to your will. We ask this through Christ our Lord. **Amen**.

Gospel (Luke 1:39-56)

Mary set out and traveled to the hill country in haste to a town of Judah, where she entered the house of Zechariah and greeted Elizabeth. When Elizabeth heard Mary's greeting, the infant leaped in her womb, and Elizabeth, filled with the Holy Spirit, cried out in a loud voice and said, "Blessed are you among women, and blessed is the fruit of your womb. And how does this happen to me, that the mother of my Lord should come to me? For at the moment the sound of your greeting reached my ears, the infant in my womb leaped for joy. Blessed are you who believed that what was spoken to you by the Lord would be fulfilled."

And Mary said: / "My soul proclaims the greatness of the Lord; / my spirit rejoices in God my Savior / for he has looked upon his lowly servant. / From this day all generations will call me blessed: / the Almighty has done great things for me, / and holy is his Name. / He has mercy on those who fear him / in every generation. / He has shown the strength of his arm, / and has scattered the proud in their conceit. / He has cast down the mighty from their thrones, / and has lifted up the lowly. / He has filled the hungry with good things, / and the rich he has sent away empty. / He has come to the help of his servant Israel / for he has remembered his promise of mercy, / the promise he made to our fathers, / to Abraham and his children forever."

Mary remained with her about three months and then returned to her home.

Brief Silence

For Reflection

God, who has "lifted up" his "lowly servant" Mary, lifts up all the lowly not only because they are faithful but because God is faithful to the promise of divine mercy. Mary's assumption of body and soul into heaven celebrates the mercy of God and the promise to us of a share in that same mercy. It is God who does great things because God has promised mercy. The great thing Mary does is say yes to being an instrument of God's promise. The great thing God does for us is invite us to share in that same promise— everlasting life.

God's kingdom is brought to completion when all are gathered into a share in eternal life. Mary's assumption—this festival—is a sign of the completion already coming about. This is why we might think of Mary's assumption as a festival of mercy: Mary "returned to her home" when she completed her mission of being an instrument of God's promise, a home that is to be with God for all eternity. The assumption is a sign of God's mercy being fulfilled. It is also a sign that our true home is with God.

✦ The Eucharist makes me into an instrument of God's promise of mercy for others. I witness to this whenever . . .

Brief Silence

Prayer

O living and loving God, the mother of your divine Son now shares in your eternal glory. Bring us to that same glory by helping us to live as faithfully as Mary. We ask this through Christ our Lord. **Amen.**

In the gospel Jesus invites us to journey to salvation through a narrow gate. Let us ask God for the grace to be faithful to this journey . . .

Prayer

Lord God, you will that all be saved and come to eternal life. Help us to avoid evil, to share worthily and eagerly at your Feast, and humbly serve our brothers and sisters in Christ. We ask this through Christ our Lord. **Amen**.

Gospel (Luke 13:22-30)

Jesus passed through towns and villages, teaching as he went and making his way to Jerusalem. Someone asked him, "Lord, will only a few people be saved?" He answered them, "Strive to enter through the narrow gate, for many, I tell you, will attempt to enter but will not be strong enough. After the master of the house has arisen and locked the door, then will you stand outside knocking and saying, 'Lord, open the door for us.' He will say to you in reply, 'I do not know where you are from.' And you will say, 'We ate and drank in your company and you taught in our streets.' Then he will say to you, 'I do not know where you are from. Depart from me, all you evildoers!' And there will be wailing and grinding of teeth when you see Abraham, Isaac, and Jacob and all the prophets in the kingdom of God and you yourselves cast out. And people will come from the east and the west and from the north and the south and will recline at table in the kingdom of God. For behold, some are last who will be first, and some are first who will be last."

Brief Silence

For Reflection

Jesus was asked in the gospel about how many would be saved. The issue, however, is not how many but *who*. Those who are saved don't merely accompany Jesus but freely choose to follow him "to Jerusalem" and all this destination entails. The door of salvation will be open only to all those who have chosen to pass through the "narrow gate" of self-surrender. As we can see, Jesus' answer is neither streamlined nor indicative of relative ease, as we like our lives to be. So, why would we choose this journey? Because the immediate destination (Jerusalem, with its promised death) is the way to a greater destination (new and eternal life).

Our salvation is a great gift from God, but it is not without cost. We must pass through the "narrow gate" of conforming ourselves to Jesus and participating in his dying and rising. Being disciples of Jesus, then, demands more than being in Jesus' company (for example, being faithful to personal prayer and celebrating liturgy); it means we must take up the mission of Jesus to die and rise, that is, we must be on the way to Jerusalem.

✦ The way I am God's food that aids and encourages others to enter through the narrow gate is . . .

Brief Silence

Prayer

Almighty God, you offer salvation to those who faithfully follow your Son. Be with us on our journey of self-giving for the good of others, that one day we may enter eternal life. We ask this through Christ our Lord. **Amen.**

Each Sunday the Body of Christ gathers to dine at the Lord's table. Let us prepare ourselves to be nourished by word and sacrament by humbling ourselves before our generous God . . .

Prayer

O good God, you invite all to your banquet of love. Help us to prepare to come to your table worthily by reaching out in humility to those in need. We ask this through Christ our Lord. **Amen**.

Gospel (Luke 14:1, 7-14)

On a sabbath Jesus went to dine at the home of one of the leading Pharisees, and the people there were observing him carefully.

He told a parable to those who had been invited, noticing how they were choosing the places of honor at the table. "When you are invited by someone to a wedding banquet, do not recline at table in the place of honor. A more distinguished guest than you may have been invited by him, and the host who invited both of you may approach you and say, 'Give your place to this man,' and then you would proceed with embarrassment to take the lowest place. Rather, when you are invited, go and take the lowest place so that when the host comes to you he may say, 'My friend, move up to a higher position.' Then you will enjoy the esteem of your companions at the table. For everyone who exalts himself will be humbled, but the one who humbles himself will be exalted." Then he said to the host who invited him, "When you hold a lunch or a dinner, do not invite your friends or your brothers or your relatives or your wealthy neighbors, in case they may invite you back and you have repayment. Rather, when you hold a banquet, invite the poor, the crippled, the lame, the blind; blessed indeed will you be because of their inability to repay you. For you will be repaid at the resurrection of the righteous."

Brief Silence

For Reflection

The word "humility" derives from the Latin adjective *humilis*, which means "on the ground, of the earth, earthy" (noun: *humus*, "ground, earth, soil"). From this we understand humility as not being someone other than we are, just down-to-earth folks who know ourselves in both our gifts and our limitations. In the gospel today, Jesus uses two very familiar social situations—dining at table and guest invitation lists—to teach us about true humility. From the point of view of being guest, humility is knowing one's place; from the point of view of being host, humility is knowing whom to invite (to be in relation with).

In the gospel the people dining with Jesus were "observing him carefully." What Jesus says turns the tables by inviting the guests to look at themselves. Jesus challenges them to choose not "a higher position" but "the lowest place," teaching us who we are to be before God and each other. Jesus calls us to true humility: to know the truth about ourselves, to sit in right relationship with one another, and to allow ourselves to be lifted up by God.

✦ My distributing Holy Communion is an example of true humility and of taking a lower place when . . .

Brief Silence

Prayer

Almighty God, you humble us by calling us to be guests at your heavenly banquet. Teach us right relationships with each other, that one day we may share forever at your heavenly banquet table. We ask this through Christ our Lord. **Amen**.

The cost of discipleship is high, as we hear in this Sunday's gospel: we must lose our lives, carry our crosses, and renounce our possessions. Jesus speaks strong words to help us understand the cost of following him. Let us pray for wisdom and the guidance of the Holy Spirit to help us be faithful . . .

Prayer

Almighty and everlasting God, your Son Jesus taught us that we must surrender ourselves if we are to be his disciples. Strengthen us to pick up our daily cross of self-sacrifice and come to new life through him. We ask this through Christ our Lord. **Amen**.

Gospel (Luke 14:25-33)

Great crowds were traveling with Jesus, and he turned and addressed them, "If anyone comes to me without hating his father and mother, wife and children, brothers and sisters, and even his own life, he cannot be my disciple. Whoever does not carry his own cross and come after me cannot be my disciple. Which of you wishing to construct a tower does not first sit down and calculate the cost to see if there is enough for its completion? Otherwise, after laying the foundation and finding himself unable to finish the work the onlookers should laugh at him and say, 'This one began to build but did not have the resources to finish.' Or what king marching into battle would not first sit down and decide whether with ten thousand troops he can successfully oppose another king advancing upon him with twenty thousand troops? But if not, while he is still far away, he will send a delegation to ask for peace terms. In the same way, anyone of you who does not renounce all his possessions cannot be my disciple."

Brief Silence

For Reflection

In this Sunday's gospel Jesus is very up front with us. He bluntly challenges the crowd to take up the demands of discipleship with eyes wide open. Jesus clearly spells out the fine print in large, large letters: disciples must put Jesus ahead of their families and even their own lives, carry their cross, and renounce all they have. Why would anyone make such a choice to be his follower? Because Jesus has shown us by his own choices that this is the only way to the fullness of life. Discipleship constantly demands of us radical and calculated choices. It offers incalculable fruits.

Jesus intends no surprises for those who choose discipleship; here's the fine print: we have to die if we wish to follow Jesus. The cost of discipleship seems disproportionately high compared to anything we could want or value as humans. And this is the point: following Jesus to Jerusalem leads us beyond human expectations. It leads to death, to be sure, but a death that grants us a share in God's very divine life, an outcome worth any price.

✦ Eucharist reveals the cost of discipleship by . . . Eucharist inspires and nourishes me to pay the price because . . .

Brief Silence

Prayer

Lord of life, you spell out the cost of discipleship as well as reveal the fruits. Help us not so much to calculate the cost of following Jesus faithfully as to anticipate the fruit of eternal life you offer us. We ask this through Christ our Lord. **Amen**.

Whenever we are lost or faltering on our Christian journey, God is there with divine compassion and love. As we take time to pray, let us open our hearts to such a lavish God . . .

Prayer

Shepherd God, you will that not one of us be lost. Reach out and touch us with your presence, that we may be encouraged to seek only you as the center of our lives. We ask this through Christ our Lord. **Amen**.

Gospel (Luke 15:1-10 [Longer Form: Luke 15:1-32])

Tax collectors and sinners were all drawing near to listen to Jesus, but the Pharisees and scribes began to complain, saying, "This man welcomes sinners and eats with them." So to them he addressed this parable. "What man among you having a hundred sheep and losing one of them would not leave the ninety-nine in the desert and go after the lost one until he finds it? And when he does find it, he sets it on his shoulders with great joy and, upon his arrival home, he calls together his friends and neighbors and says to them, 'Rejoice with me because I have found my lost sheep.' I tell you, in just the same way there will be more joy in heaven over one sinner who repents than over ninety-nine righteous people who have no need of repentance.

"Or what woman having ten coins and losing one would not light a lamp and sweep the house, searching carefully until she finds it? And when she does find it, she calls together her friends and neighbors and says to them, 'Rejoice with me because I have found the coin that I lost.' In just the same way, I tell you, there will be rejoicing among the angels of God over one sinner who repents."

Brief Silence

For Reflection

Whether a child is lost a short time or a long time, the anguish of the parents is the same until their child is found. It is heartrending to see notices of people who have been missing for many years. Seeking the lost is something we humans do out of deep compassion and love. Even when a total stranger is lost, we take notice. How often, for example, when a toddler strays into woods, hundreds of people turn up as soon as news is out to begin the search. And what rejoicing occurs when someone is found! If this is so true of us as humans, how much more true is it of our loving God! In this Sunday's gospel Jesus uses parables to tell us how much God seeks us when we are lost, how much God (and all of heaven!) rejoices when we are found.

No calculating person would risk ninety-nine or nine for one, or have a feast for one who has squandered so much. No one today would turn a house upside down to find a lost penny (we probably wouldn't even know we lost it). But God does not act like us calculating humans—God always acts with the utmost compassion and love.

✦ My ministry embodies Jesus' compassion and love for others in that . . .

Brief Silence

Prayer

Rejoicing God, you seek us even when we stray from your loving presence. Help us always to recognize your love and care, and never to turn from you. We ask this through Christ our Lord. **Amen**.

In this gospel Jesus reminds us that we cannot serve both God and money. We must make a choice. Let us open our hearts to encounter Jesus, who helps us make good choices as his followers . . .

Prayer

Almighty God, you call us to turn to you as the very center of our lives. Help us to make the choice to serve you and you alone. We ask this through Christ our Lord. **Amen**.

Gospel (Luke 16:10-13 [Longer Form: Luke 16:1-13])

Jesus said to his disciples, "The person who is trustworthy in very small matters is also trustworthy in great ones; and the person who is dishonest in very small matters is also dishonest in great ones. If, therefore, you are not trustworthy with dishonest wealth, who will trust you with true wealth? If you are not trustworthy with what belongs to another, who will give you what is yours? No servant can serve two masters. He will either hate one and love the other, or be devoted to one and despise the other. You cannot serve both God and mammon."

Brief Silence

For Reflection

We must handle the things of this world and our daily actions in relation to what is eternal and with prudent decisiveness. This means that there can be no split between our spiritual/religious lives (for example, going to Mass on Sunday) and our daily living. Christianity is better expressed as a *way of life* than as practices to be fulfilled. Prudent decisiveness about our future means that "religion" is an expression of our relationship to God that is shown in the simple choices of our daily living. To put it simply, prudent decisiveness about our future means that God is truly at the center of our lives. Truly, we serve God and God alone.

When it comes to gospel living, we often squander opportunities to serve God alone. The thrust of the gospel is that we act prudently in this life in order to gain eternal life. Prudence demands that we not squander opportunities to be charitable and just toward others. Prudence demands that we not squander opportunities to die to self. Prudence demands that we not squander opportunities to be trustworthy with the ministry of discipleship, which we take on each time we say yes to serving God alone.

✦ My manner of distributing Holy Communion reveals that God is the center of my life in that . . .

Brief Silence

Prayer

Everlasting God, you call us to serve you with undivided hearts. Help us to be trustworthy so that one day we may enjoy everlasting life with you. We ask this through Christ our Lord. **Amen**.

Let us open ourselves to God's presence and prepare to listen to God's word, that we may respond to others with generosity and compassion . . .

Prayer

Compassionate God, you give us every opportunity to know what is right and to care for others as you have cared for us. Help us to be truthful and right in our choices to put the good of others ahead of ourselves. We ask this through Christ our Lord. **Amen**.

Gospel (Luke 16:19-31)

Jesus said to the Pharisees: "There was a rich man who dressed in purple garments and fine linen and dined sumptuously each day. And lying at his door was a poor man named Lazarus, covered with sores, who would gladly have eaten his fill of the scraps that fell from the rich man's table. Dogs even used to come and lick his sores. When the poor man died, he was carried away by angels to the bosom of Abraham. The rich man also died and was buried, and from the netherworld, where he was in torment, he raised his eyes and saw Abraham far off and Lazarus at his side. And he cried out, 'Father Abraham, have pity on me. Send Lazarus to dip the tip of his finger in water and cool my tongue for I am suffering torment in these flames.' Abraham replied, 'My child, remember that you received what was good during your lifetime while Lazarus likewise received what was bad; but now he is comforted here, whereas you are tormented. Moreover, between us and you a great chasm is established to prevent anyone from crossing who might wish to go from our side to yours or from your side to ours.' He said, 'Then I beg you, father, send him to my father's house, for I have five brothers, so that he may warn them, lest they too come to this place of torment.' But Abraham replied,

'They have Moses and the prophets. Let them listen to them.' He said, 'Oh no, father Abraham, but if someone from the dead goes to them, they will repent.' Then Abraham said, 'If they will not listen to Moses and the prophets, neither will they be persuaded if someone should rise from the dead.'"

Brief Silence

For Reflection

This Sunday's gospel is a parable about the needy at our door with an admonition to *listen*. We are so inundated with requests for donations that we can turn a deaf ear to them; it is so easy to live oblivious to the needs of others. Jesus makes clear at the end of this parable, however, that we are given everything we need to set our values and relationships right. We have the words of "Moses and the prophets." Even more, unlike the rich man in the parable, we *do* have Someone among us who has "rise[n] from the dead." We need only to listen. This is how we gain the insight to see those in need at our own door and choose how to respond.

There is a great "chasm" between selfishness and self-surrender, between evil and good, between the lost and saved. This chasm is a metaphor for *listening* to God's word and allowing ourselves to be guided by its demands. The time to respond decisively to God and others is *now*; after death it is too late.

✦ When I distribute Holy Communion, I am "listening" to the needs of others in that . . .

Brief Silence

Prayer

Dear God, we are the needy at your door whom you never turn away. Help us to extend the same generosity and kindness to our neighbors, to listen and respond to their needs, and to treat them with dignity and honor. We ask this through Christ our Lord. **Amen**.

We pray for the faith to remain decisive in following Jesus. Let us open ourselves to God's presence so that our faith may grow stronger . . .

Prayer

Lord, you always hear the prayer that rises from sincere hearts. Increase our faith; help us to be faithful servants; help us to do good. We ask this through Christ our Lord. **Amen**.

Gospel (Luke 17:5-10)

The apostles said to the Lord, "Increase our faith." The Lord replied, "If you have faith the size of a mustard seed, you would say to this mulberry tree, 'Be uprooted and planted in the sea,' and it would obey you.

"Who among you would say to your servant who has just come in from plowing or tending sheep in the field, 'Come here immediately and take your place at table'? Would he not rather say to him, 'Prepare something for me to eat. Put on your apron and wait on me while I eat and drink. You may eat and drink when I am finished'? Is he grateful to that servant because he did what was commanded? So should it be with you. When you have done all you have been commanded, say, 'We are unprofitable servants; we have done what we were obliged to do.'"

Brief Silence

For Reflection

In this Sunday's gospel the apostles ask Jesus to "increase [their] faith." What he gives them instead is greater confidence in the power of the faith they already have. What is this faith? It is obedience to responsibility, a matter of willingness to undertake decisive action for the sake of God's kingdom. Even faith that "feels" small possesses great power. In the gospel when Jesus suggests that a little bit of faith can move a mulberry tree, he's not suggesting that we hire hydraulic equipment! He's suggesting that we recognize that the power to be faithful disciples is not found in "how much" but in how obedient we are to responsibility.

Faithfulness is doing all we have been commanded. "Faith-filledness" is *acting* decisively. The faithful and faith-filled disciple is the one who doesn't wait for enough faith, but continues to respond to the everyday and never-ending demands of discipleship. The Master demands our service. And then gives us the faith to perform it well.

✦ Distributing the Eucharist strengthens my faith in that . . .

Brief Silence

Prayer

God of faith, hope, and love, you are present in all we do. Increase our faith so that one day we may enjoy everlasting life with you. We ask this through Christ our Lord. **Amen**.

In the gospel only one leper returns to Jesus to give thanks for being healed. As we prepare to share in the eucharistic feast, let us open our hearts in gratitude for God's presence and healing power . . .

Prayer

Gracious God, your Son Jesus gave us his Body and Blood as a thanksgiving feast. Help us to recognize the gifts of healing, faith, and nourishment that you offer us each day, and to always raise grateful hearts to you. We ask this through Christ our Lord. **Amen**.

Gospel (Luke 17:11-19)

As Jesus continued his journey to Jerusalem, he traveled through Samaria and Galilee. As he was entering a village, ten lepers met him. They stood at a distance from him and raised their voices, saying, "Jesus, Master! Have pity on us!" And when he saw them, he said, "Go show yourselves to the priests." As they were going they were cleansed. And one of them, realizing he had been healed, returned, glorifying God in a loud voice; and he fell at the feet of Jesus and thanked him. He was a Samaritan. Jesus said in reply, "Ten were cleansed, were they not? Where are the other nine? Has none but this foreigner returned to give thanks to God?" Then he said to him, "Stand up and go; your faith has saved you."

Brief Silence

For Reflection

One leper is very different from the other nine, although all are healed. He alone returned to Jesus to give thanks for being healed. But the gospel is telling us even more: the leper's return revealed a depth of faith that Jesus acknowledged as a sign of salvation ("your faith has saved you"). This faith led him to turn from the command of Jesus ("Go show yourselves to the priests"), which would have fulfilled the ancient law concerning restoration of lepers to the community. Instead, the Samaritan leper returns to the source of his healing. Jesus is not only the One who healed him of his leprosy but more important, he is the One who drew him to act on the faith that assured him of the new life of restoration and salvation. Faith is discovering who Jesus is; salvation is the life-long journey of returning to and encountering him. In the gospel, encounter with Jesus leads to the declaration "your faith has saved you." Salvation is not freedom from disease but relationship with Christ.

✦ While distributing Holy Communion, I witness others coming to Jesus in faith. This deepens my faith in that . . .

Brief Silence

Prayer

God of the nations, in your love there is no foreigner, no one excluded from salvation. Increase our faith and gratitude, and may they lead us to everlasting life with you. We ask this through Christ our Lord. **Amen**.

Jesus calls us to be persistent in prayer. Let us pray ardently and open ourselves to God's merciful, healing presence . . .

Prayer

Lord God, you are just and full of mercy. Hear our prayer for mercy and just judgment, that we may journey faithfully as followers of your Son Jesus. We ask this through Christ our Lord. **Amen**.

Gospel (Luke 18:1-8)

Jesus told his disciples a parable about the necessity for them to pray always without becoming weary. He said, "There was a judge in a certain town who neither feared God nor respected any human being. And a widow in that town used to come to him and say, 'Render a just decision for me against my adversary.' For a long time the judge was unwilling, but eventually he thought, 'While it is true that I neither fear God nor respect any human being, because this widow keeps bothering me I shall deliver a just decision for her lest she finally come and strike me.'" The Lord said, "Pay attention to what the dishonest judge says. Will not God then secure the rights of his chosen ones who call out to him day and night? Will he be slow to answer them? I tell you, he will see to it that justice is done for them speedily. But when the Son of Man comes, will he find faith on earth?"

Brief Silence

For Reflection

Persistence in prayer is not only about asking for what we need now but is also about maintaining hope that God will persist in bringing about final justice. Moreover, there is no real prayer without faith. Faith gives prayer a longer view and a broader vision—the view and vision of Jesus himself. In this, Jesus is teaching us that while our prayer tends to be about immediate needs, our life is about ultimate justice. Our persistence in prayer really is about a faith relationship with God that reveals we are God's "chosen ones" who are in right relationship with God. This righteousness leads to eternal life.

The gospel's legal language of judge, judgment, and justice brings to mind the final judgment that Jesus renders at his Second Coming. One way to prepare for this Second Coming and to alleviate any fears we might have is to be persistent in faith-filled prayer. When Jesus comes again, "will he find faith on earth?" Yes, if we are persistent in praying "always without becoming weary." It seems persistence in prayer is a small price to pay for salvation and everlasting glory!

✦ As I distribute Holy Communion to each one who comes, my persistent prayer is . . .

Brief Silence

Prayer

Just and merciful God, you hear the persistent and faith-filled prayers of those who cry out to you. Secure us as your chosen ones and lead us to everlasting life. We ask this through Christ our Lord. **Amen**.

Jesus contrasts the prayer of the proud Pharisee with that of the humble tax collector. We now humbly open our own hearts to God's mercy . . .

Prayer

Merciful God, you are pleased with the humble of heart who turn to you in sincerity and truth. Hear our cries for mercy, help us acknowledge our sinfulness, and heal us of all that keeps us from you. We ask this through Christ our Lord. **Amen**.

Gospel (Luke 18:9-14)

Jesus addressed this parable to those who were convinced of their own righteousness and despised everyone else. "Two people went up to the temple area to pray; one was a Pharisee and the other was a tax collector. The Pharisee took up his position and spoke this prayer to himself, 'O God, I thank you that I am not like the rest of humanity—greedy, dishonest, adulterous—or even like this tax collector. I fast twice a week, and I pay tithes on my whole income.' But the tax collector stood off at a distance and would not even raise his eyes to heaven but beat his breast and prayed, 'O God, be merciful to me a sinner.' I tell you, the latter went home justified, not the former; for whoever exalts himself will be humbled, and the one who humbles himself will be exalted."

Brief Silence

For Reflection

In the parable the Pharisee's prayer is praise for himself that he is "not like the rest of humanity." The tax collector, on the other hand, identifies himself with all of humanity as a sinner in need of God's mercy. The former is taken up with what he does for God (fasts, pays tithes). The latter is overcome by awareness of what he needs from God (mercy). The Pharisee justified himself; the tax collector "went home justified" by God. Jesus tells us that we are "justified" when we know who we are before God and open ourselves in humility to receive God's mercy.

Justification is knowing who God is and what our relationship to God is. It is addressing God as God and letting God be God. It is acknowledging humbly who we are before God: sinners in need of mercy. The exaltation at the end of time is determined by whether we are justified, that is, humble and in right relationship with God. Good works alone don't justify us—it is right relationship with God. Humility in the face of our all-holy and merciful God brings exaltation.

✦ My distributing Holy Communion keeps me humble because . . .

Brief Silence

Prayer

Exalted God, you hear the prayers of those who come humbly before you. Increase the depth of our honest prayer to you, and lead us to the fullness of life this brings. We ask this through Christ our Lord. **Amen**.

In this familiar gospel episode Zacchaeus climbs a tree in order to see Jesus. Let us open our hearts to encounter Jesus in the ordinary circumstances of our daily lives, and to be changed by his presence . . .

Prayer

God of salvation, no sin is so great and no weakness is so draining that you do not seek and save. Help us to see your goodness and presence all around us, and heal us of our infirmities. We ask this through Christ our Lord. **Amen**.

Gospel (Luke 19:1-10)

At that time, Jesus came to Jericho and intended to pass through the town. Now a man there named Zacchaeus, who was a chief tax collector and also a wealthy man, was seeking to see who Jesus was; but he could not see him because of the crowd, for he was short in stature. So he ran ahead and climbed a sycamore tree in order to see Jesus, who was about to pass that way. When he reached the place, Jesus looked up and said, "Zacchaeus, come down quickly, for today I must stay at your house." And he came down quickly and received him with joy. When they all saw this, they began to grumble, saying, "He has gone to stay at the house of a sinner." But Zacchaeus stood there and said to the Lord, "Behold, half of my possessions, Lord, I shall give to the poor, and if I have extorted anything from anyone I shall repay it four times over." And Jesus said to him, "Today salvation has come to this house because this man too is a descendant of Abraham. For the Son of Man has come to seek and to save what was lost."

Brief Silence

For Reflection

Zacchaeus finds himself up the proverbial tree—both physically and metaphorically. In this gospel episode Zacchaeus is the epitome of the despised person—chief tax collector, wealthy, a sinner. And yet he is the one person in the crowd in whose house Jesus chooses to stay. Encountering Jesus does not depend upon goodness of life, but it can bring about conversion of life: Zacchaeus undergoes dramatic change (he sets his affairs right and gives to the poor). His newfound concern for others is a sign of encounter with Jesus, who brings salvation. Our own encounters with Jesus can bring about just as dramatic a change in our lives. We need only to be willing to go to ever greater heights to "see him."

Zacchaeus is the last person Luke's gospel mentions before Jesus enters Jerusalem—it is as though Luke saves the worst for last in order to make his point: "For the Son of Man has come to seek and to save what was lost." If even for this sinner "salvation has come," then who would ever be excluded?

✦ As I distribute Holy Communion, I see others encounter Jesus. This changes me in that . . .

Brief Silence

Prayer

Almighty God, you exclude no one from your plan of salvation. Help us to respond to your grace, receive the life you offer, and come to eternal life. We ask this through Christ our Lord. **Amen**.

At our baptism we were blessed by God and made children of God. May we remain faithful to our baptismal promises, as were the saints whom we honor today . . .

Prayer

Holy God, we praise your name and thank you for your gift of grace. Help us to be faithful to your will, as were the saints we honor this day. We ask this through Christ our Lord. **Amen**.

Gospel (Matt 5:1-12a)

When Jesus saw the crowds, he went up the mountain, and after he had sat down, his disciples came to him. He began to teach them, saying: / "Blessed are the poor in spirit, / for theirs is the Kingdom of heaven. / Blessed are they who mourn, / for they will be comforted. / Blessed are the meek, / for they will inherit the land. / Blessed are they who hunger and thirst for righteousness, / for they will be satisfied. / Blessed are the merciful, / for they will be shown mercy. / Blessed are the clean of heart, / for they will see God. / Blessed are the peacemakers, / for they will be called children of God. / Blessed are they who are persecuted for the sake of righteousness, / for theirs is the Kingdom of heaven. / Blessed are you when they insult you and persecute you and utter every kind of evil against you falsely because of me. Rejoice and be glad, for your reward will be great in heaven."

Brief Silence

For Reflection

Throughout their lives the saints faithfully opened themselves to the transforming action of Christ within them. This transforming action strengthened their identity as God's children and enabled them to embody the Beatitudes as a way of living. For us who share this same identity and way of living, our reward will not only be with the saints in heaven but is already on earth: we are even now blessed by God and bathed in comfort, mercy, and peace. The paradox of the Beatitudes is that we already *are* what we try to live: those blessed by God.

The saints stand out as models who give us courage and strength so that we, too, can be faithful to the demands of the way of living the Beatitudes laid out for us. We know some saints by name (those who have been canonized). There are countless others (our deceased relatives and friends) whom we know by name in a different way. This multitude of faithful followers of Christ beckons us to hear what Jesus teaches in this gospel: "Blessed are [you] . . . your reward will be great in heaven."

✦ The impact that the saints have on my faith life is . . . Saints I know are . . .

Brief Silence

Prayer

Ever-faithful God, you bless us with every good thing. Keep us faithful and holy, that one day we may join all the saints in offering you everlasting praise in heaven. We ask this through Christ our Lord. **Amen**.

We pray for the faithful departed, who are our beloved brothers and sisters in Christ. Let us open ourselves to the Good News that Jesus, who has conquered death, will raise us up on the last day . . .

Prayer

Almighty and eternal God, you love us and offer us salvation. Hear our prayers for the faithful departed, that they may enjoy everlasting peace with you. We ask this through Christ our Lord. **Amen**.

Gospel (John 6:37-40 [see page 125 for other Gospel options])

Jesus said to the crowds: "Everything that the Father gives me will come to me, and I will not reject anyone who comes to me, because I came down from heaven not to do my own will but the will of the one who sent me. And this is the will of the one who sent me, that I should not lose anything of what he gave me, but that I should raise it on the last day. For this is the will of my Father, that everyone who sees the Son and believes in him may have eternal life, and I shall raise him up on the last day."

Brief Silence

For Reflection

This festival commemorating the faithful departed is a popular one among many people. It is also comforting, reassuring, and hope-filled. It is comforting in that Jesus rejects no one the Father has given to him and raises to new life those who have been buried with him in baptism. It is reassuring in that the faithful followers of Jesus share in everlasting life. It is hope-filled because it "is the will" of the Father that anyone who believes in Jesus will "have eternal life." We celebrate this festival confident of the Good News that our beloved faithful departed are within the embrace of God.

The only thing that can separate anyone from Christ and sharing in everlasting life is to refuse to follow Jesus into his death. Our deceased loved ones are awaiting the fullness of life with Jesus. This festival reminds us to be faithful in our own call to follow Jesus so that one day we will share in his fullness of life. It's not death that is the worst of things; it's being separated from Jesus.

✦ What gives me hope that one day I will be with Jesus forever in heaven is . . .

Brief Silence

Prayer

Ever-living and loving God, you graciously offer us everlasting life. Keep us faithful, help us to surrender ourselves to your holy will, and bring us to eternal life. We ask this through Christ our Lord. **Amen**.

Other Gospel options for November 2:
Matthew 5:1-12a / Matthew 11:25-30 / Matthew 25:31-46 / Luke 7:11-17 / Luke 23:44-46, 50, 52-53; 24:1-6a / Luke 24:13-16, 28-35 / John 5:24-29 / John 6:51-58 / John 11:17-27 / John 11:32-45 / John 14:1-6

Jesus promises everlasting life to those who are faithful. Let us open ourselves during our prayer to the living God who comes to save . . .

Prayer

God of Abraham, Isaac, and Jacob, you raise the dead to new life. Strengthen us to be alive in your Son, faithful followers of his law of love, and seekers of eternal life. We ask this through Christ our Lord. **Amen**.

Gospel (Luke 20:27, 34-38 [Longer Form: Luke 20:27-38])

Some Sadducees, those who deny that there is a resurrection, came forward.

Jesus said to them, "The children of this age marry and re-marry; but those who are deemed worthy to attain to the coming age and to the resurrection of the dead neither marry nor are given in marriage. They can no longer die, for they are like angels; and they are the children of God because they are the ones who will rise. That the dead will rise even Moses made known in the passage about the bush, when he called out 'Lord,' the God of Abraham, the God of Isaac, and the God of Jacob; and he is not God of the dead, but of the living, for to him all are alive."

Brief Silence

For Reflection

Resurrection is much more than simply a theological issue worthy of debate. Resurrection is a way of living, witnessing to our belief that there is more to life than what meets the eye. The basis for this belief is *hope*. Although hope always has a future orientation about it, when we have confidence in God's grace to bring about change in us and when we have patience with ourselves while that change comes about, we already have something of the future in the present—we already are living this new, risen life that is characterized by faithful relationship with God. The relationship enabled by risen life is that of being "children of God" in an everlasting relationship with the living God.

With the promise of risen life, the suffering we face now seems like nothing in comparison. In order for this to be really true for us, we must have zeal for God and God's ways that are, for us, a way of living. God is a God of the living. This is the core of our hope, borne out by the daily choices we make to be faithful followers of Jesus.

✦ The manner of my distributing Holy Communion helps others realize that they are participating in the new life Jesus brings when . . .

Brief Silence

Prayer

Loving God, we are your children coming to you confident in your offer of salvation. Hear our prayers for faithfulness and lead us in the way everlasting. We ask this through Christ our Lord. **Amen**.

The gospel invites us not to look to cosmic events such as wars, earthquakes, and famine for signs of the end of the world, but to look to the faithfulness of our own discipleship. Let us pray for perseverance . . .

Prayer

God of hope and confidence, you preserve your faithful ones for everlasting life. May we persevere in our witness to the Good News, not be discouraged by opposition and ridicule, and remain faithful to the name we bear. We ask this through Christ our Lord. **Amen**.

Gospel (Luke 21:5-19)

While some people were speaking about how the temple was adorned with costly stones and votive offerings, Jesus said, "All that you see here—the days will come when there will not be left a stone upon another stone that will not be thrown down."

Then they asked him, "Teacher, when will this happen? And what sign will there be when all these things are about to happen?" He answered, "See that you not be deceived, for many will come in my name, saying, 'I am he,' and 'The time has come.' Do not follow them! When you hear of wars and insurrections, do not be terrified; for such things must happen first, but it will not immediately be the end." Then he said to them, "Nation will rise against nation, and kingdom against kingdom. There will be powerful earthquakes, famines, and plagues from place to place; and awesome sights and mighty signs will come from the sky.

"Before all this happens, however, they will seize and persecute you, they will hand you over to the synagogues and to prisons, and they will have you led before kings and governors because of my name. It will lead to your giving testimony. Remember, you are not to prepare your defense beforehand, for I myself shall give you a wisdom in speaking that all your adversaries will be powerless to resist or refute. You will even be handed over by parents, brothers, relatives, and friends, and they will put some of you to death. You will be hated by all because of my name, but not a hair on your head will be destroyed. By your perseverance you will secure your lives."

Brief Silence

For Reflection

The signs of the end time that Jesus names (wars, insurrection, earthquakes, famine, plagues, etc.) describe human history as it has *always* been. Jesus assures us that the end is not immediate. The challenge for us as faithful followers is to face persecution with courage *now*, testify to Jesus' name *now*, open ourselves *now* to the wisdom given us by Jesus. Embracing this way of living gives us hope and confidence that, no matter when the end time comes, our lives are secure.

We might ask, then, what will be so different at the end time? In one sense every day is already the beginning of the end time. The signs we observe of human calamities bid us to testify to all that Jesus taught us—that there is more to life than we can see. We must live faithfully *now*. By our perseverance as faithful followers testifying to Jesus' name, we secure everlasting life. Every day is an opportunity to live discipleship fully and confidently. Every day is an opportunity to grow in our relationship with Jesus, the One who promises life to his faithful ones.

✦ Like the gift of the Eucharist itself, my ministry offers others strength, courage, and hope by . . .

Brief Silence

Prayer

God of promises, you assure us that your Son will come to bring judgment, but you also assure us of salvation for the faithful ones. Be with us in our daily struggles and help us to remain faithful to the Gospel. We ask this through Christ our Lord. **Amen.**

As we prepare ourselves to celebrate the end of this liturgical year, let us ask Christ our King to strengthen our resolve to imitate him through a life of self-giving for the good of others . . .

Prayer

Saving God, we exalt your Son Jesus as Christ our King. May we always live his Gospel and witness to the fullness of life it offers. We ask this through Christ our Lord. **Amen**.

Gospel (Luke 23:35-43)

The rulers sneered at Jesus and said, "He saved others, let him save himself if he is the chosen one, the Christ of God." Even the soldiers jeered at him. As they approached to offer him wine they called out, "If you are King of the Jews, save yourself." Above him there was an inscription that read, "This is the King of the Jews."

Now one of the criminals hanging there reviled Jesus, saying, "Are you not the Christ? Save yourself and us." The other, however, rebuking him, said in reply, "Have you no fear of God, for you are subject to the same condemnation? And indeed, we have been condemned justly, for the sentence we received corresponds to our crimes, but this man has done nothing criminal." Then he said, "Jesus, remember me when you come into your kingdom." He replied to him, "Amen, I say to you, today you will be with me in Paradise."

Brief Silence

For Reflection

By naming Christ our "King," we acknowledge him and his way of living as the wellspring of our goodness and salvation. We acknowledge our status as his "subjects," called to relate to others as he did. We acknowledge our shared inheritance as the "holy ones" (second reading) who receive life through him. By naming Christ our King we identify him as the One who offers us the fullness of life in his kingdom both now and forever. By naming Christ our King we also accept the responsibility to be faithful to the demands required of those who follow him. This is the relationship to which the image "king" challenges us: we are our King's "kin." We inherit from him what is his to give: life. That inheritance has its cost.

Although Jesus' kingdom is established from the very beginning of creation and through the Davidic kingship, his reign is not one of power but of mercy, not one of self-service but of self-giving, not one of material wealth but of eternal salvation. His throne is a cross. Such a King the world has never seen.

✦ When I distribute Holy Communion, I am drawn to think about Christ as my King when . . .

Brief Silence

Prayer

O God who rules and saves, prompt our hearts to hail your Son as Christ our King, inviting him to reign in our hearts now and forever. We ask this through Christ our Lord. **Amen**.